CRIME AND PUNISHMENT

CRIME AND PUNISHMENT

A PLAY IN THREE ACTS

by

FRANK J. MORLOCK

From the Novel by Fyodor Dostoyevsky

THE BORGO PRESS

An Imprint of Wildside Press LLC

MMIX

www.wildsidepress.com

FIRST WILDSIDE EDITION

CONTENTS

DEDICATION

To

DAGNY (JACKIE STANTON)

Without whose invaluable assistance this play (and several others) would have remained permanently in manuscript and never seen the light of day.

CAST OF CHARACTERS

Marmeldov
Raskolnikov
The Bartender
The Student
The Officer
Dounia
Razumihin
Zametov
Porfiry Petrovitch
The Man
Sonya
Svidrigailov

ACT I

SCENE 1

A TAVERN

There are several tables. There is a bartender, Marmeldov, Raskolnikov, and several students.

MARMELDOV: (to Raskolnikov) Excuse me, sir, but may I venture to engage you in polite conversation? I can see at once you are a gentleman. And I, too, am a civil servant. Marmeldov; Marmeldov, such is my name. Are you a civil servant, too?

RASKOLNIKOV: No, I am a student.

MARMELDOV: I knew it. I knew it at once. My experience in affairs told me at once. But all—

RASKOLNIKOV: Thank you.

MARMELDOV: Tell me; just out of curiosity. Have you

ever spent a night on a hay barge on the Neva River?

RASKOLNIKOV: Are you trying to insult me? Be careful.

MARMELDOV: No, no, no, honored, sir. I did not mean to imply. On the contrary. It's just that I've spent my fifth night there. (solemnly) Sir, poverty is not a vice. That's true enough. But drunkenness is not a virtue, either. But beggary, beggary, sir,(loudly) IS A VICE. Hence, the pothouse. You understand what I mean?

BARTENDER: He's a riot. (to Marmeldov) Why aren't you working if you're a civil servant? Today's Monday.

MARMELDOV: (to Raskolnikov) Why am I not on duty, as it were? Why am I not on duty, sir? Because I am worthless. Worthless. A week ago, Mr. Lebeziatnikov beat my wife while I lay there drunk. Oh, I tell you how I suffered. (guffawing from everyone present, except Raskolnikov who does not laugh)

MARMELDOV: Tell me young man, have you ever petitioned hopelessly for a loan? I mean when you knew in advance that on no consideration will you obtain your object?

RASKOLNIKOV: Yes. That's happened to me.

MARMELDOV: After all, why should he give it to me? Of course, he knows I shan't pay it back. Nonetheless, I go to him.

RASKOLNIKOV: But why? Why humiliate yourself?

MARMELDOV: Well, when one has no one, where else can one go? Everyone must have somewhere to go. Because—because there are times when one absolutely must go somewhere. As an example, when my daughter was forced to register as a prostitute.—No matter, sir, no matter.

(There are more guffaws.)

RASKOLNIKOV: How can you expose yourself and her in this way?

MARMELDOV: Expose myself? I am exposed already. Everyone knows about it. I am humble. So be it. So be it. Behold the man. Excuse me, young man. Can you or rather dare you, looking upon me, assert that I am not a pig?

(Silence.)

MARMELDOV: Well, so be it. I am a pig. But my wife, Katerina, she is a lady. I have the semblance of a pig, but she is a general's daughter. But although she is magnanimous, she is unjust. When she pulls my hair, she does it only out of pity. Such is my fate. (more guffawing) I am a beast by nature.

BARTENDER: Amen.

MARMELDOV: I've sold her clothes for drink. Her very shoes and stockings. And she, poor thing, has consumption. I feel it. Do you suppose I don't feel it? And when I drink, I feel it more. That's why I drink. So that I may suffer twice as much.

BARTENDER: Well, that's a new one. (guffaws)

MARMELDOV: (to the whole room) What do any of you know? (returning to Raskolnikov) Young man, I seem to see trouble in your face. I am looking for a man of feeling and education who can understand what it is for a general's daughter to marry a pig like me. Her first husband was a gambler, and he abandoned her and her three children. And then I, a widower, with a daughter of my own, offered her my hand. She would never have accepted me if she hadn't been starving.

RASKOLNIKOV: But why are you telling me all this? You can see for yourself that I can't help you.

MARMELDOV: Do you understand what it is when someone has nowhere to turn? No, you don't understand yet. For a whole year, I performed my duties faithfully and didn't touch a drop. Then I lost my job through no fault of my own. Then we made our way to Petersburg. And do you know what? I obtained a situation, and lost it again. This time it was my own fault because of my weakness.

RASKOLNIKOV: Hadn't you better stop for a while?

MARMELDOV: No, no. I must drink. I must tell you. And meanwhile my daughter grew up. Katerina Ivanovna, though generous, is spirited and irritable. She would say to my daughter, How can you live with us and do nothing to help? Do you suppose a respectable girl can earn any money? Ah, I was lying drunk at the time and I heard my Sonia say, Am I really to do a thing like that? Katerina said, And why not? You are something precious to be careful of? Ah, but I don't blame her. Do you blame her, sir? Do you?

RASKOLNIKOV: She shouldn't have said that.

MARMELDOV: I can't blame her. Don't blame her. She was not herself. She has consumption. Sonia went out. When she came back, she gave thirty roubles to Katerina without a word. Katerina kissed her feet. And I lay drunk.

RASKOLNIKOV: Are you sure this is good for you to be talking like this?

MARMELDOV: And now, she has been made to register as a prostitute and they won't let Sonia stay at our house. Do you hear? They threw her out of our house because she is a prostitute. Well, I got a new job, and everything was fine till a week ago when I stole the key to Katerina's box and took out her earnings. I've been drunk ever since. This morning, I went to Sonia for money, hee, hee, hee.

SOMEONE ELSE: Do you mean to say she gave it to you?

MARMELDOV: Of course. She is a good daughter. She said nothing. Ah, in heaven they grieve over men, they don't blame them. She is an angel. Tell me, do you pity men of my sort? Are you sorry for me or not?

BARTENDER: What are you to be pitied for?

(Guffaws and laughter.)

MARMELDOV: Ah, that is the question. I ought to be crucified. Oh, but if you crucify me, pity me. On judgment day, God will call even drunkards forth and pity us. He will do it because they didn't believe themselves worthy of being pitied. (Marmeldov falls unconscious)

SOMEONE: That's his notion.

BARTENDER: Well, I guess we'd better throw him out.

RASKOLNIKOV: No, don't, I'll take him when I'm ready to go.

BARTENDER: All right, Mr.—?

RASKOLNIKOV: Raskolnikov.

(The Bartender nods and moves Marmeldov to a bench by the wall. At the next table, a student and an officer are seated.)

OFFICER: I say, Nikolai. I've got to pawn some stuff. A debt of honor, you understand. Do you know anyone who—?

NIKOLAI: Of course. A student always knows a good pawnbroker. Hey, Mr. Raskolnikov?

RASKOLNIKOV: I'm afraid it's true.

NIKOLAI: What do you say to Alyosha Ivanovna?

RASKOLNIKOV: (nods his head) I've made use of her.

NIKOLAI: She's first rate. You can always get money from her. But if you're a day late with your interest, she'll foreclose. She's old, too. Very old. And she's got a sister that she treats like a servant and beats her like a child.

RASKOLNIKOV: What's so strange about that?

NIKOLAI: Nothing, except that Alyosha is a small woman and her sister Lizaveta stands an inch over six feet.

RASKOLNIKOV: What does her sister do? I never knew she had one.

NIKOLAI: She makes clothes.

OFFICER: Is that so? Would you send her around to my place tomorrow? I could use some work done.

ANOTHER STUDENT: You know what beats all is that this Lizaveta is hideous. And she's constantly pregnant.

OFFICER: But how can that be if she's so ugly.

NIKOLAI: People are attracted to ugliness these days. But she's gentle and has sweet eyes. I imagine those who like her are those who want to degrade themselves.

OFFICER: You seem to find her attractive yourself.

NIKOLAI: Maybe. I tell you what. I could kill that damned old woman and make off with her money without the slightest remorse.

RASKOLNIKOV: That's a strange thing to say. I hope you were joking.

NIKOLAI: Of course, I'm joking. But seriously, on the one hand we have a stupid, spiteful, ailing, horrid, worthless old woman; a woman not just useless, but doing a great deal of harm, you understand. And she will die very soon anyway. You see the point?

OFFICER: I understand.

NIKOLAI: Well, listen then. Fresh young lives, by the thousands, thrown away for want of help. A hundred thousand good deeds could be done on that woman's money. Hundreds might be saved from destitution, from ruin, from vice. Kill her, take her money and with the help of it dedicate oneself to humanity.

RASKOLNIKOV: You propose communism?

NIKOLAI: Nothing of the sort. I am simply suggesting that one might really benefit mankind by murder of this sort. Morality is sometimes prejudiced. One little crime would be wiped away in the benefits arising to the community.

RASKOLNIKOV: What you say is very strange.

NIKOLAI: Why is it strange?

RASKOLNIKOV: Because I have had similar thought.

NIKOLAI: You see! Of what value is a life like that anyway, in Nature's scheme? No more than a louse. Do you know she is positively doing harm? The other day she nearly broke Lizaveta's back.

OFFICER: Of course, she doesn't deserve to live. But there it is; it's Nature.

NIKOLAI: But we are learning to correct Nature. Otherwise we should be drowned in an ocean of prejudice.

But for that, there shouldn't have been a single great man. They talk of duty, of conscience. I have nothing against duty and conscience—but after all, what do they mean?

RASKOLNIKOV: You mean you believe a great man has the right to commit crime?

NIKOLAI: Of course.

RASKOLNIKOV: You shouldn't say things like that. That's revolution.

NIKOLAI: Wait. I have another question to ask you.

RASKOLNIKOV: You wait. I've a question to ask you first. Listen.

NIKOLAI: Well?

RASKOLNIKOV: You are talking and ranting away. But tell me: would you kill the old woman yourself?

NIKOLAI: Of course not. I was only considering the abstract justice of it. If it came to what I, personally, would do—

RASKOLNIKOV: But I think, if you would not do it yourself, there's no justice about it—

NIKOLAI: I was trying to be objective about it, that's all.

RASKOLNIKOV: But all morality is subjective. If you won't do a thing yourself, how can you say someone else should?

OFFICER: Ah, you philosophers. What I am concerned with is getting my coat mended. Send Lizaveta to me tomorrow night, Nikolai.

RASKOLNIKOV: (musing) The old woman will be all to herself. It would be an ideal time to put your theory into action, Nikolai.

NIKOLAI: Ah, don't be absurd. But I still think it's a good idea.

OFFICER: Are you ready to go, Mr. Raskolnikov? We'll help you with your friend, if you like.

RASKOLNIKOV: Thanks, I could use it. He looks rather heavy.

(They go to Marmeldov and prop him up.)

BLACKOUT

ACT I

SCENE 2

RASKOLNIKOV'S GARRET

When the curtain goes up Raskolnikov is seen working on his coat. He has tied a noose inside under one of the arms. He looks at it. He pulls the noose to be sure it is secure. From the table he takes an ax. He puts the ax through the noose. He removes the ax, puts the coat on, then replaces the ax in the noose. He inspects it with great care to determine whether the ax is visible or not. Satisfied he removes the ax and then the coat. There is a knock. He stands petrified.

RASKOLNIKOV: Just a minute! (slipping the coat onto the chair and hiding the ax under the bed) Come in.

(Dounia, his sister enters; she is slightly younger than Raskolnikov.)

RASKOLNIKOV: Dounia!

DOUNIA: Rodya, darling.

RASKOLNIKOV: Dearest sister. How is mother?

DOUNIA: She is very well.

RASKOLNIKOV: But, what are you doing in Petersburg? I thought you were working as a governess in Moscow.

DOUNIA: I was.

RASKOLNIKOV: Well then?

DOUNIA: Can't we talk about pleasanter things?

RASKOLNIKOV: Dounia, what's wrong?

DOUNIA: Nothing's wrong.

RASKOLNIKOV: Then why are you in Saint Petersburg?

DOUNIA: I came to see you.

RASKOLNIKOV: Is that the only reason?

DOUNIA: N-no.

RASKOLNIKOV: Then stop beating around the bush and tell me.

DOUNIA: Well, you see, I'm going to get married.

RASKOLNIKOV: Really? Well, that's wonderful. Who is the lucky man? Why haven't you written me about it?

DOUNIA: Well, it's a rather sudden decision.

RASKOLNIKOV: Dounia, what's all this mystery about? Who are you going to marry?

DOUNIA: I'm going to marry Mr. Luzhin, the attorney.

RASKOLNIKOV: But he's no match for you. He's twice your age and besides, I know him to be a totally worthless fellow.

DOUNIA: Please don't say things like that about my future husband.

RASKOLNIKOV: You'd be much better off as a governess with the Svidrigailovs.

DOUNIA: I can't go back there.

RASKOLNIKOV: You mean you threw over a good position to marry that—that pompous little worm, Luzhin. I thought you were happy at the Svidrigailovs?

DOUNIA: I was.

RASKOLNIKOV: Then why can't you go back?

DOUNIA: It's impossible, that's all. Madame Svidrigailov is dead. She died six weeks ago.

RASKOLNIKOV: Still. It would seem your presence would be more necessary now than before.

DOUNIA: It's not that.

RASKOLNIKOV: I thought you loved the children.

DOUNIA: I do.

RASKOLNIKOV: Then why must you leave? You aren't going to pretend you're in love with Mr. Luzhin?

DOUNIA: I respect Mr. Luzhin. But you see I can't go back—because I was insulted.

RASKOLNIKOV: What!

DOUNIA: I didn't want to tell you, but now I see I must. Everything was fine at the beginning. Madame Svidrigailov was kind; the children were adorable. Mr. Svidrigailov was reserved. He seemed to dislike me. But he was polite. He avoided me whenever he could. And that is how things stood until about ten weeks ago. Then, Mr. Svidrigailov began approaching me more and more often. I thought at first I should make friends with him and was very pleased. But it soon became apparent he wanted to be more than friends.

RASKOLNIKOV: Ah, the scoundrel.

DOUNIA: I will say this for him. I sincerely believe that he loved me. I was not just an adventure. He finally proposed that we run off together. Rodya, he's frightening. He's capable of anything. I was indignant, but I thought he would leave me alone. But no; he pestered me all the time. Finally, Madame Svidrigailov overheard him one day, and unwilling to put the blame where it belonged, blamed me. I was thrown out of the house.

RASKOLNIKOV: Ah, this is horrible, horrible.

DOUNIA: There was a terrible scene. Then afterwards she spread gossip all over town. I could hardly have gotten a new position. But finally, Madame Svidrigailov learned the truth and she repented publicly in church. She managed to reestablish my good name and she set about to make atonement. She conceived the idea of this match between myself and Mr. Luzhin, who is a cousin of hers.

RASKOLNIKOV: Ah, I knew there was something behind it. You wouldn't have chosen him by yourself.

DOUNIA: Please, Rodya.

RASKOLNIKOV: And Madame Svidrigailov is dead?

DOUNIA: Yes. And—Rodya, the worst part is, I'm sure

Svidrigailov murdered her.

RASKOLNIKOV: What?

DOUNIA: I can't prove it, of course. I just know, though. He's fully capable of it and he was furious with her for attacking me, and then preventing him by arranging this match with Mr. Luzhin.

RASKOLNIKOV: So he is a free spirit, too.

DOUNIA: The cause of death was said to be natural, but I will never believe it.

RASKOLNIKOV: Well, what difference can it make to you?

DOUNIA: A great deal. You see he asked me to marry him before she was even cold in her grave. He took advantage of the fact that I went to the funeral.

RASKOLNIKOV: You don't mean to say that—?

DOUNIA: I find him very attractive, although I am not in love with him. But I can't marry him with suspicions like these.

RASKOLNIKOV: But you can marry Luzhin?

DOUNIA: He's acceptable. He's offered me an honorable situation.

RASKOLNIKOV: He's a pompous ass.

DOUNIA: He's a trifle conceited. But, after all, being conceited is not a vice.

RASKOLNIKOV: He's too old for you.

DOUNIA: He's still in his early forties. It's not an un-heard of difference, even in love matches.

RASKOLNIKOV: He's stupid.

DOUNIA: He's very good natured.

RASKOLNIKOV: You don't love him.

DOUNIA: I will make him a very dutiful wife. He said that he meant to marry a poor, but well brought up girl because he regards it as bad for a man to marry for money and be indebted to his wife.

RASKOLNIKOV: Oh, I see. So he can force his wife to respect him. To worship him for marrying her. That's his reason. The dog!

DOUNIA: I don't think he meant it that way, Rodya. It's his nature to want to protect the weak and the helpless, that's all.

RASKOLNIKOV: Bah! He's afraid of a woman who has any self respect. He knows she wouldn't respect him.

DOUNIA: Rodya, dear, don't talk like that without meeting him. You will meet him; you won't sulk?

RASKOLNIKOV: Very well. I shall meet him. But, I promise you, I shan't like him.

DOUNIA: Oh, Rodya, just think. You can be his partner. You've studied law. Now you'll be able to finish your studies and—

RASKOLNIKOV: So, you're doing this for me.

DOUNIA: I'm doing what I wish to do.

RASKOLNIKOV: Well, I won't have it.

DOUNIA: I shall decide this for myself.

RASKOLNIKOV: And mother? Does she approve?

DOUNIA: Of course.

RASKOLNIKOV: How much of this was put into words between you? You sacrifice yourself, and she will let you. Well, I won't have it.

DOUNIA: I wish you'd try to understand.

RASKOLNIKOV: I don't wonder at mother; she'd say a goose was a swan until the very last minute. But you, Dounia? You turn down Svidrigailov and then you agree to become Luzhin's legal concubine? You won't do anything for your own advantage, but for mine you'd sacrifice everything. Maybe you even persuade yourself that what you're doing is not prostitution just the same.

DOUNIA: Rodya, I beg you to stop.

RASKOLNIKOV: I will not stop. Do you know I met a man yesterday whose daughter became a prostitute to save the family from starvation? And what good does it do? They will starve in the end anyway. And you'd do the same thing. And let me tell you, this Sonya's fate is no worse than life with Mr. Luzhin. This degradation has to be paid for. It has to be paid for.

DOUNIA: I'll go and come back some other time. You're not yourself.

RASKOLNIKOV: Don't go, Dounia. Dounia, I don't want your sacrifice. I won't permit it as long as I shall live. I won't! I won't have it!

DOUNIA: (angry at last) You won't have it? You forbid it? And what right have you? What can you offer on your side to give you such a right? You will devote your life to us, I suppose, when you finish your studies and obtain your post? When will that be? We've heard all that before. And that's all words. But now? Now something must be done! Now, do you understand that? And what can you do now? You are living on us. How are you going to save me from Svidrigailov, O future millionaire brother? In ten years mother will be blind knitting shawls, and I'll be an old maid who cannot get a man if she wants one. (bursting into tears)

RASKOLNIKOV: What you say is very true. I am useless to everyone right now.

DOUNIA: Oh, Rodya, I am sorry, I didn't mean it.

RASKOLNIKOV: But it's true, Dounia. I'm pulling you down, not lifting you up. I'm dependant on you. And what do I do? I sit here reading books. I don't even do that anymore. How can I prevent you from marrying him, even if I want to? (looking at a bust of Napoleon, then at his coat) But perhaps, I am not completely helpless. Perhaps I shall do something. If I have the courage.

DOUNIA: (sniffs) Don't be angry with me, darling.

RASKOLNIKOV: I'm not angry with you. I'm angry with myself. But I shall do something. If I have the courage.

DOUNIA: What will you do?

RASKOLNIKOV: A job.

DOUNIA: Will you give lessons again?

RASKOLNIKOV: That's chickenfeed. Besides, I have to be well dressed to give lesson.

DOUNIA: Then, what?

RASKOLNIKOV: An idea, that's all.

DOUNIA: Anyway, I can give you a little money to get some new clothes.

RASKOLNIKOV: No, Dounia. I don't want it.

DOUNIA: I insist.

RASKOLNIKOV: I won't take your money.

DOUNIA: Well, at least, let me mend your coat while I'm here.

RASKOLNIKOV: (shouting) Don't touch my coat.

DOUNIA: Really, Rodya, you're very nervous today.

RASKOLNIKOV: I'm sorry.

DOUNIA: And I don't see why you're so dead set against my marriage. Weren't you about to marry your land-lady's daughter about a year ago? And you would have, too, but for the fact she died.

RASKOLNIKOV: That's all over with.

DOUNIA: Yes, because she died. She was indescribably ugly. You were willing to sacrifice yourself for us.

RASKOLNIKOV: That's another matter.

DOUNIA: (ready to go) Will you accompany me to my lodgings?

RASKOLNIKOV: What time is it?

DOUNIA: Nearly six.

RASKOLNIKOV: I'm not sure I can. I have an appointment at seven. Where are you staying?

DOUNIA: In the Mirograd Prospekt.

RASKOLNIKOV: What? Why, that's a terrible neighborhood. Didn't the noble Mr. Luzhin give you any money?

DOUNIA: He didn't think it proper. He only paid the fare.

RASKOLNIKOV: The cheap swine.

DOUNIA: He wasn't being cheap. He merely wanted things to look right

RASKOLNIKOV: Look right. Keep up appearances.

DOUNIA: Let's not start all over again.

(A knock.)

RASKOLNIKOV: Who can that be? I never have any visitors.

(He opens the door and admits Razumihin.)

RAZUMIHIN: Ah, Rodion Romanovitch, where have you been hiding? I'd heard of a translating job I thought I could put you in the way of. (abashed, seeing Dounia) Oh! I didn't know you had company.

RASKOLNIKOV: This is my sister, Adovtya Romanovna.

RAZUMIHIN: Very pleased to meet you.

RASKOLNIKOV: Dounia Darling, I want you to meet Mr. Razumihin; a fellow student and a good friend of mine.

DOUNIA: (very gracious) I'm delighted.

RAZUMIHIN: I really didn't intend to stay. (he is obviously very uncomfortable in her presence)

RASKOLNIKOV: Then, perhaps, you can do me the favor of accompanying my sister home. I have an appointment that I simply must keep, and I shan't have time.

RAZUMIHIN: But, do you really think I should? I mean, she won't be offended, will she? What shall I say to her?

RASKOLNIKOV: Why, Razumihin, I thought you were a man of the world?

RAZUMIHIN: Well, after all—

RASKOLNIKOV: He's shy, sister. The big oaf is shy.

DOUNIA: I really would like an escort. I'm new to Petersburg and I don't know my way very well.

RAZUMIHIN: Why, of course. It's not that I don't want to.

DOUNIA: You see, I've come to be married.

RAZUMIHIN: Oh. (sighing with disappointment)

DOUNIA: Goodnight, brother.

RAZUMIHIN: Goodnight.

RASKOLNIKOV: Don't get lost. Goodnight. I shall see you both in the morning. We must discuss this again, Dounia.

(They leave. Waiting until he is sure he is alone, Raskolnikov puts on his coat, and carefully removes the ax from under the bed. He puts the ax securely in the noose. Then he approaches the portrait of Napoleon.)

RASKOLNIKOV: (addressing the bust) And why should I not? Why should I not? Would you hesitate? What is a life to you? Or thousands even? Millions? But can I do it? Of course not. This is only an experiment. Granted there is no flaw in the reasoning. Still, shall I be able to? No, it will only be an experiment. An experiment.

(Carefully brushing his coat to be sure the ax does not show, he walks out.)

CURTAIN

ACT II

SCENE 3

RASKOLNIKOV'S GARRET

A week later, night.

After the curtain rises, on the grimy wall by the bust of Napoleon, a series of slides flash on the wall before the lights go up:

1st. A Russian peasant drinking.
2nd. A picture of the peasant and a horse-drawn sleigh. The peasant is beckoning his friends.
3rd. The friends climbing onto the sleigh.
4th. The sleigh is overloaded.
5th. The horse is not pulling the sleigh.
6th. The peasant beating the horse.
7th. The horse being kicked by the peasant.
8th. a repeat of picture 6.
9th. A repeat of picture 7.
10th. A picture of the peasant's enraged face.
11th. A picture of an ax.

12th. A picture of the peasant with an ax.

13th. A picture of the peasant striking the horse with the ax.

14th. A repeat of picture 10.

15th. A repeat of picture 13.

16th. A slide covered with blood.

17th. A repeat of 11.

18th. A picture of a bloodstained sock.

19th. A repeat of 16.

The lights go up. It is morning in Raskolnikov's garret. Raskolnikov wakes up, dazedly he begins to look for something. First he looks in the closet.

RASKOLNIKOV: Where is it? (he begins going around on all fours.) I must find that sock. (peeping under the bed) Damn. If anyone should find it. Where is it? (becoming increasingly frantic he looks under the bed clothes and begins tearing the sheets and covers off the bed) Where is that sock? It's all covered with blood. Must find it. Must find it and destroy it.

(A loud knock on the door. Raskolnikov trembles. He quickly piles things on the bed. Razumihin enters.)

RAZUMIHIN: Whatever are you doing?

RASKOLNIKOV: I—I was just looking for my sock.

RAZUMIHIN: Shall I help?

RASKOLNIKOV: No! No point! I was going to lie down again, anyway.

RAZUMIHIN: So the patient is better today?

RASKOLNIKOV: Patient? What are you talking about?

RAZUMIHIN: You've been sick for a week, Rodion.

RASKOLNIKOV: How long have you been coming here?

RAZUMIHIN: Why, I told you all about it this morning. Don't you remember?

RASKOLNIKOV: No. How long have I been delirious?

RAZUMIHIN: Since the morning after I met your sister here for the first time. You were ill that morning, and went to the police station, against all good advice.

RASKOLNIKOV: (nervous) The Police Station? Why did I do a thing like that?

RAZUMIHIN: Because you were summoned.

RASKOLNIKOV: What for?

RAZUMIHIN: By your landlady to pay your rent.

RASKOLNIKOV: (relieved) Oh, is that all?

RAZUMIHIN: You really have been in a bad way. I can see I've been playing the fool again with all my chatter. I thought to amuse you and I've only made you cross.

RASKOLNIKOV: Was I delirious long?

RAZUMIHIN: A week.

RASKOLNIKOV: Did I say anything in my delirium?

RAZUMIHIN: I should think so! You were beside yourself

RASKOLNIKOV: What did I rave about?

RAZUMIHIN: What do people rave about? Everything.

RASKOLNIKOV: (insisting) What did I rave about?

RAZUMIHIN: Are you afraid of having let out a guilty secret? Don't worry yourself. You talked, oh, let's see, about earrings, about a noose. Yes, and about your sock. That was of special interest to you. You wanted your sock. You were still looking for it when I got here just now.

RASKOLNIKOV: Good God. (then he laughs)

RAZUMIHIN: What are you laughing about?

RASKOLNIKOV: I just remembered what I did with my

sock.

RAZUMIHIN: Eh, what?

RASKOLNIKOV: I destroyed it.

RAZUMIHIN: That explains why you couldn't find it. Now look, dear boy, I promised your sister—

RASKOLNIKOV: Has she been here—?

RAZUMIHIN: All the time. It was all I could do to prevent her from moving in. She comes during the day, and I come during the night. But she must sleep, poor thing.

RASKOLNIKOV: Yes, of course.

RAZUMIHIN: If you're well enough tomorrow, will you come to my party? I'm having a little housewarming.

RASKOLNIKOV: Well—who will be there?

RAZUMIHIN: Zametov will. And let's see—

RASKOLNIKOV: Zametov? What have you to do with him?

RAZUMIHIN: Zametov's a nice fellow.

RASKOLNIKOV: Zametov takes bribes.

RAZUMIHIN: Well, what of it? I don't praise him for it. I only say, for all that, he's a nice man. Put any of us under a microscope, and who won't be found crawling? I'm sure I wouldn't be worth more than a baked onion, myself.

RASKOLNIKOV: I still don't see what you have in common.

RAZUMIHIN: Well, right now, we are working on a case together—

RASKOLNIKOV: A case?

RAZUMIHIN: Yes. There's a student named Nikolai Afasnyovich. You know him by sight, don't you?

RASKOLNIKOV: Yes.

RAZUMIHIN: Well, we're trying to get him out of a jam. Of course, he'll get out anyway, but—

RASKOLNIKOV: What's it all about?

RAZUMIHIN: Ah, didn't I tell you this morning? No. I didn't. And you'd have forgotten anyway. Well, he's mixed up in the murder of this pawnbroker.

RASKOLNIKOV: Who?

RAZUMIHIN: Alyona Ivanovna.

RASKOLNIKOV: When did all this happen?

RAZUMIHIN: The night I met your sister here.

RASKOLNIKOV: Ah.

RAZUMIHIN: Lizaveta was murdered, too.

RASKOLNIKOV: Lizaveta?

RAZUMIHIN: Yes. She sold old clothes. Don't you remember her? She used to come here to mend for you?

RASKOLNIKOV: I was just thinking. How horrible.

RAZUMIHIN: First, the police pitched on the house-painters.

RASKOLNIKOV: Oh. Did the murderers use an ax?

RAZUMIHIN: Yes. How did you know?

RASKOLNIKOV: I—

RAZUMIHIN: Oh, you must have heard about it when you went to the police station the next morning.

RASKOLNIKOV: Yes. Things are coming back to me. I heard of it while I was at the police station.—Is there any evidence against Nikolai?

RAZUMIHIN: Some, but he clearly didn't do it. You see, he had a set of earrings that belonged to her. The person who pawned them was able to identify them. Nikolai claims he came to ask Lizaveta to do some mending for an officer friend. He planned to go around seven, but he didn't get there until seven thirty. The downstairs door was open. He walked in. Seeing the earrings behind the door he decided to make off with them

RASKOLNIKOV: Still, that's evidence.

RAZUMIHIN: Circumstantial! Circumstantial!

RASKOLNIKOV: Enough to send a man to Siberia.

RAZUMIHIN: There's worse. The night before he was in a tavern and was heard to plot the crime aloud.

RASKOLNIKOV: Well, how do you explain it then?

RAZUMIHIN: It was nonsense, of course. He was simply talking about the justice of killing her and taking her money. Conversations like that are a dime a dozen. Surely, no one who planned a murder would talk about it so openly. That's proof he didn't do it.

RASKOLNIKOV: Perhaps. But will a court think so? And, how do you explain the earrings?

RAZUMIHIN: Very simple. The murderer was standing behind the door and dropped them when he realized he was trapped.

RASKOLNIKOV: It's no good, Razumihin.

RAZUMIHIN: Why not?

RASKOLNIKOV: Because it all fits together too well. It's too logical and melodramatic.

RAZUMIHIN: Bah.

(The door opens and Luzhin enters.)

LUZHIN: (to Razumihin) Rodion Romanovitch Raskolnikov; a student or formerly a student?

RAZUMIHIN: There he is on the sofa. What do you want?

RASKOLNIKOV: Yes, I am Raskolnikov.

LUZHIN: Pyotr Petrovitch Luzhin, I think my name is not unknown to you.

RASKOLNIKOV: I—I don't seem to remember.

LUZHIN: Is it possible, you don't know who I am? I thought—I was given to understand that you had been informed—

RAZUMIHIN: Say, why are you standing in the doorway? If you've got something to say come in and sit down. No need to be nervous. Rodya's been delirious for the last week, I am a comrade. Take no notice of me—

LUZHIN: Your sister—

RASKOLNIKOV: I know, I know! So you are the fiancé. I know and that's enough.

LUZHIN: I just arrived in town, but I was sure she had told you and I came to see you directly.

RASKOLNIKOV: She did, but I forgot. I am not quite clear about what has happened this last week. (staring at him)

LUZHIN: (uncomfortable) Ah, if I had been aware of your illness, I should have come earlier. But I've been in Moscow on very serious business.

RASKOLNIKOV: Why did you take lodgings for her in Vokeressenky in Bakaleyev's house?

LUZHIN: Why, because it was near your rooms.

RASKOLNIKOV: It's a cheap filthy place. I've been there. What's more, it's of doubtful character.

LUZHIN: But—

RASKOLNIKOV: It's cheap, though.

LUZHIN: I could not, of course, know much about that, as I am a stranger here myself. However, the rooms are exceedingly clean. I have taken our future flat and am having it done up. Meanwhile, I am staying with my friend Andrey Semyonovitch Lebziatnikov. It was on his advice that I took the lodgings.

RASKOLNIKOV: Lebziatnikov?

LUZHIN: Do you know him?

RASKOLNIKOV: Was he the one who beat Marmeldov's wife?

LUZHIN: I shall certainly ask him. It sounds unlikely. He's a very nice young man. One learns a lot from the young today.

RAZUMIHIN: How do you mean?

LUZHIN: Oh, well, in the provinces we get all the novelties, but to really see the changes, we must come to Petersburg. And, it is my notion, you will see most by watching the young. I am delighted, I confess.

RAZUMIHIN: At what?

LUZHIN: At their practicality.

RAZUMIHIN: (flying at him) Nonsense! They're not practical at all. Ideas, if you like, are fermenting, and desire for good exists. But practicality, no, not that.

LUZHIN: (pleasantly, enjoying an argument in which he hopes to shine) I disagree. To be sure, the young get carried away with enthusiasm; but one must be indulgent. The main thing is that the old prejudices have been destroyed forever. We've made a clean cut with the past, and that, to my thinking, is a great thing.

RASKOLNIKOV: (under his breath) He learned that speech by heart to show off.

LUZHIN: (not catching his words) What? Anyway, take economics for example. They told us to love thy neighbor. What came of it? I tear my coat in half to share with him and we both go half-naked. Now we know that rational self interest is better than philanthropy. It's a simple truth, but it has been obscured by idealism and philanthropy.

RAZUMIHIN: Let's drop it. I've grown sick of these bull sessions. No doubt you want to exhibit your talents, and I don't blame you, that's quite pardonable. I only wanted to find out what sort of man you are. So many scoundrels have got hold of the progressive cause of late, that it's been dragged in the mud. Let's drop it.

LUZHIN: Excuse me, Sir. But do you mean to suggest that I, too—

RAZUMIHIN: Oh, my dear sir, how could I? Come; that's enough. The subject is distasteful to me, that's all.

LUZHIN: (to Raskolnikov) I trust our acquaintance will become closer. Above all, I hope for your return to health.

RAZUMIHIN: Have you heard about the murder?

LUZHIN: Ah, yes. I heard about it in the neighborhood. What is our society coming to?

RASKOLNIKOV: Why worry about it? It's in accordance with your theory.

LUZHIN: In accordance with my theory?

RASKOLNIKOV: Surely. Rational self interest and to hell with everyone else.

LUZHIN: There's a measure in all things. Economic ideas are not an incitement to murder.

RASKOLNIKOV: And, is it true you told your fiancée that what pleased you most was that she was a beggar? Because it's better to raise a wife from poverty so that you may have complete control over her by being her benefactor.

LUZHIN: Good God! To distort my words like that! Let me say that there's no foundation to that interpretation at all, and I suspect who—

RASKOLNIKOV: Who—?

LUZHIN: It was not your sister; it must have been your mother, although I scarcely believed she would so misunderstand me or represent me in so fanciful a way.

RASKOLNIKOV: I tell you what, I tell you what—

LUZHIN: What?

RASKOLNIKOV: If ever you dare mention a single word about my mother, I'll throw you downstairs.

RAZUMIHIN: What is the matter with you?

LUZHIN: So that's how it is! Let me tell you, sir. I saw from the first moment that you were hostile to me, but I stayed to find out why. I could forgive a great deal from a sick man and a relative; but you,—Never after this!

RASKOLNIKOV: I am not ill.

LUZHIN: So much the worse.

RASKOLNIKOV: Go to hell!

RAZUMIHIN: How could you? How could you?

(Luzhin leaves.)

RASKOLNIKOV: Let me alone, let me alone, will you! Will you ever leave off tormenting me? Go away. I want to be alone, alone, alone.

RAZUMIHIN: But, how can I leave you like this?

RASKOLNIKOV: Oh, if you won't go, then I will.

RAZUMIHIN: But, your sister?

RASKOLNIKOV: Damn her! She's the cause of everything.

RAZUMIHIN: Have you lost your mind?

(A knock.)

RASKOLNIKOV: Come in.

RAZUMIHIN: Zametov.

ZAMETOV: How is the patient today?

RAZUMIHIN: That's a doctor's entering line, not a policeman's.

ZAMETOV: So who's a policeman? I'm just a police clerk. How are you, Rodion Romanovitch?

RASKOLNIKOV: Oh, all right, I suppose.

RAZUMIHIN: Look, can you stay here with him while I fetch his sister?

RASKOLNIKOV: There's no need.

RAZUMIHIN: Yes, there is a need. Now don't argue, Rodya.

RASKOLNIKOV: You're impossible to deal with. Impossible.

RAZUMIHIN: It's only a step. I'll be back in no time. (he hurries out)

ZAMETOV: Razumihin told me yesterday you were delirious.

RASKOLNIKOV: Yes, that's true. I hear you're cooperating with Razumihin.

ZAMETOV: Ah, yes. We must save that innocent boy Nikolai.

RASKOLNIKOV: You, too, think he's innocent.

ZAMETOV: He's much too nice a fellow to commit a bloodthirsty crime like that. Do you know, there was blood all over the place? All over the place! He had bashed their skulls with an ax.

RASKOLNIKOV: (weakly) I think Nikolai innocent, too.

ZAMETOV: Are you sure you should be up? You seem unwell.

RASKOLNIKOV: Oh, do I seem strange to you?

ZAMETOV: Yes, as a matter of fact. I can't help thinking you're still delirious.

RASKOLNIKOV: You think me delirious, do you? You are fibbing, my little friend. You find my behavior suspicious? Confess, my boy, you'd like to know what it is that's making me so nervous?

ZAMETOV: Well, what is it?

RASKOLNIKOV: Aha. How you prick up your ears. Well, I'll tell you. I confess—no, that's not the right word, I depose that I am upset by the murder of the old woman.

ZAMETOV: Well, that's no business of mine.

RASKOLNIKOV: Perhaps, I know something about it.

ZAMETOV: Well, if you do, why don't you tell?

RASKOLNIKOV: (mysteriously) Perhaps, I don't dare.

ZAMETOV: You are either mad or—

RASKOLNIKOV: Or? Or what? What? Come, tell me!

ZAMETOV: Nothing. It's all nonsense. (pause) There have been many such crimes lately. Only the other day I read about some counterfeiters in Moscow.

RASKOLNIKOV: So you consider them criminals?

ZAMETOV: Of course.

RASKOLNIKOV: I know about them. They were simpletons, children, not criminals. They used untrustworthy persons to change their forgeries. What a thing to do: trust strangers! And then, even if they made millions, they'd be dependant on each other for the rest of their lives. Do you know how they were caught? Because one of the men who changed the notes trembled as he was counting out the bills and stuffed the money in his pockets and ran away. The whole thing went crash because of one fool! Is it possible?

ZAMETOV: Ah, yes, it's true. Sometimes one cannot stand things.

RASKOLNIKOV: Stand what?

ZAMETOV: Why, could you stand it then? I wouldn't have the nerve, would you?

RASKOLNIKOV: I'd count the notes backwards and forward. Then I'd hold them up to the light to check for counterfeits. I'd put the cashier in such a stew he's do most anything to get rid of me.

ZAMETOV: What terrible things you say.

RASKOLNIKOV: Bah!

ZAMETOV: But all that is only talk. I dare say, when it came to deeds, you'd make a slip. Even a desperate man cannot always count on himself; much less you and I. Take, for example, our murderer.

RASKOLNIKOV: Why don't you catch him then?

ZAMETOV: We will. We will.

RASKOLNIKOV: Who? You? Do you suppose you will catch him? Ha, ha, ha. A big thing for you is whether a man is spending money or not. If he has no money and suddenly begins spending money, then he must be the man. A child could mislead you.

ZAMETOV: The fact is, they all do that. They usually wind up in a tavern. They are not all as clever as you. You wouldn't go to a tavern, would you?

RASKOLNIKOV: (frowning) You seem to enjoy the subject; would you like to know how I should behave in that case?

ZAMETOV: I should like to.

RASKOLNIKOV: Very much?

ZAMETOV: Very much.

RASKOLNIKOV: Very well. This is what I would do. (staring him in the face) I'd take the money and go straight to some deserted place. A churchyard, perhaps. I'd look for a stone I'd seen undisturbed for some time. Then, I'd hide the money and jewels right there and not go near it for a year or two. Let them search. There'd be no trace.

ZAMETOV: You are a madman.

RASKOLNIKOV: And, what if it was I who murdered the old woman?

ZAMETOV: That's impossible.

RASKOLNIKOV: Own up. You believed it. Yes, you did.

ZAMETOV: No. Now less than ever.

RASKOLNIKOV: Ha, ha. I've caught you. How can you believe it less than ever if you didn't believe it before?

ZAMETOV: Not at all. Have you been frightening me so as to lead up to this?

RASKOLNIKOV: You don't believe it then? Here, would you like to see my money? Where did I get it? Don't tell me you haven't been wondering? It's all very suspicious, isn't it? Perhaps I found buried treasure.

(A knock on the door.)

RASKOLNIKOV: Come in.

(A little man of comic proportions enters; he is bald but for two tufts of flabby hair.)

PORFIRY: Rodion Romanovitch Raskolnikov?

RASKOLNIKOV: Yes.

PORFIRY: Allow me to introduce myself. Porfiry Petrovitch, Inspector of Police.

RASKOLNIKOV: (to Zametov) You see. They've come to get me.

ZAMETOV: This is a surprise.

PORFIRY: Ah, Zametov, you here. I didn't know Raskolnikov was your friend, or I should have asked you to attend to this.

RASKOLNIKOV: What can I do for you?

PORFIRY: It's about the case of Alyona Ivanovna.

ZAMETOV: Good lord!

RASKOLNIKOV: What about it?

PORFIRY: I thought you might have some information.

RASKOLNIKOV: Why should you think that?

PORFIRY: You mean you don't know?

RASKOLNIKOV: No.

PORFIRY: Strange; I should have thought—. Well—

RASKOLNIKOV: Please explain.

PORFIRY: You have doubtless heard that the student Nikolai has been arrested for the crime?

RASKOLNIKOV: Only this morning. I've been ill.

PORFIRY: Oh. For how long?

RASKOLNIKOV: Since last Monday.

PORFIRY: That would be the morning after the murder. Then, you couldn't have heard earlier.

RASKOLNIKOV: What help can I be?

PORFIRY: We've learned that the night before the murder he was in a tavern and spoke openly of committing the crime.

RASKOLNIKOV: Yes.

PORFIRY: You were present and in conversation with him, were you not?

ZAMETOV: (to Raskolnikov) So that's what you meant.

RASKOLNIKOV: Yes, I was—

PORFIRY: Well, then—

RASKOLNIKOV: I am not an informer.

PORFIRY: Of course not. But it's your public duty to give a deposition.

RASKOLNIKOV: I'd rather not.

PORFIRY: Did Nikolai discuss the idea of killing the woman in your presence?

RASKOLNIKOV: Yes, he did. But only in an abstract way. When I asked him if he would do it himself, he said, of course not.

PORFIRY: Very well. That will all go in your statement. If you don't care to come to my office, I can come around and take it from you in a day or so. There's no rush now that I know what you will say.

RASKOLNIKOV: Very well.

ZAMETOV: You know he was being very mysterious about this murder just now, fancied he had some inside knowledge, but the idea seemed too fantastic.

RASKOLNIKOV: (to Zametov) Yes, I really was having fun with you. (to Porfiry) Look. I wonder if you can help me. I have some things in pawn with Alyona Ivanovna, and I should like to redeem them.

PORFIRY: You have to write a letter to the police, that such and such belong to you, and that you desire to redeem them.

RASKOLNIKOV: That's just it, at the moment I am not quite in—funds. I should like—

PORFIRY: That's no problem. You can, if you wish, write directly to me.

RASKOLNIKOV: On an ordinary sheet of paper?

PORFIRY: (ironic) Oh, the plainest sort.

RASKOLNIKOV: I thought there must be some form. Although these items are only worth a few roubles, I prize them. You may laugh at me, but my sister has come to Petersburg, and if she knew they were lost, she would be in despair. You know how women are.

PORFIRY: Oh, your sister is with you?

RASKOLNIKOV: Yes.

PORFIRY: When did she arrive?

RASKOLNIKOV: Sunday night.

PORFIRY: Actually your things are in no danger of being lost. I've been expecting you to come forward for some time.

ZAMETOV: What? But, how did you know the pledges were his?

PORFIRY (to Raskolnikov) Your things, the ring and the watch, were wrapped together with your name on them.

RASKOLNIKOV: How observant you are. I mean, there must be many pledges.

PORFIRY: It's simply that you are the only one who hasn't come forward.

RASKOLNIKOV: I haven't been very well.

PORFIRY: So I heard. You still look pale. As though you'd had a frightening experience.

RASKOLNIKOV: (snappishly) I am not pale at all. I am quite well now.

ZAMETOV: Not very well. Why only this morning he

was delirious.

PORFIRY: Really delirious? You don't say so.

RASKOLNIKOV: Nonsense! Don't you believe it! But, you don't believe it anyway. Forgive me, we're boring you, aren't we?

PORFIRY: Oh, no. Quite the contrary, quite the contrary! If you only knew how you interest me. It's interesting to look on and listen. And I am really glad you've come forward at last.

RASKOLNIKOV: Why so extraordinarily interested in me?

PORFIRY: Because you are a criminologist of sorts.

RASKOLNIKOV: I beg your pardon?

PORFIRY: I read your article "On Crime," in the *Philosophical Review*. I recognized the name at once.

RASKOLNIKOV: Ah, that. Yes, I wrote an article, but really, I didn't know it had been published.

PORFIRY: Well, they must surely owe you some money. It's a fact, I assure you.

ZAMETOV: Well, well. I didn't know you were an author. Good heavens, I shouldn't have ventured to argue with you.

RASKOLNIKOV: But, just a minute, I only signed with an initial. How did you know who wrote it?

PORFIRY: Ah, I know the editor and I asked him recently.

RASKOLNIKOV: To tell the truth, I don't quite remember what I had to say. Something about the psychology, before and after.

PORFIRY: That was not the part that interested me. Oh, it was very good; you maintained that the criminal mind is diseased. But, what really struck me, was an idea that you didn't develop fully.

RASKOLNIKOV: What was that?

PORFIRY: The suggestion that there are certain people who have a perfect right to commit crime.

ZAMETOV: What? Because of the environment, I suppose. (to Raskolnikov) You must be a socialist.

PORFIRY: On the contrary, on the contrary. The idea is rather striking, but it's hardly socialist. In his article, men are divided into ordinary and extraordinary types. Ordinary types must submit to the law, because they are ordinary. But the extraordinary are empowered to commit any crime, any transgression, because they are extraordinary. (to Raskolnikov) That was your idea, if I am not mistaken.

ZAMETOV: He can't have said that.

RASKOLNIKOV: Not quite. (to Porfiry) Although, your statement is not really a distortion. I didn't mean that extraordinary people are obligated to break the law; I merely hinted that such persons have a duty to decide whether to obey the law or not to fulfill their ideas. The laws constrict and confine extraordinary men far more than other men, and being extraordinary they are more likely to take a critical attitude towards anything that confines them. In short, you really can't stop them. Then, I point out that the laws are often in need of revision. Anyone who wants to give a new law to mankind must find himself in opposition to the existing law.

ZAMETOV: But, that doesn't give him the right to commit crime.

RASKOLNIKOV: He may not have to. There may be perfectly legal ways. Well and good. But, if he cannot find a lawful way, then, it follows, if he is to be true to himself, he must be a criminal. Take Newton and Kepler. Suppose their discoveries could not have been made without the sacrifices of a dozen or a hundred men. I maintain that Newton would have had the right, indeed have had the duty, to eliminate those men. But, it doesn't follow he would have been able to slaughter people at his whim.

ZAMETOV: Hmm. Well, how do you know they will observe this limitation?

RASKOLNIKOV: You don't, of course. And it's very common for great men to confuse their whims with the causes they stand for. But that's tyranny, of course. Yet we still admit the legitimate ruler has the right to eliminate some forms of opposition. The more devoted they are to their ideas, the more likely they will act responsibly. A whimsical fellow probably hasn't much to contribute anyway.

ZAMETOV: But, think what would come of this?

RASKOLNIKOV: What indeed? I'm only describing everyday reality. The masses will never admit this right, and will execute them whenever they can.

PORFIRY: Yes. But they are not always executed. On the contrary—

RASKOLNIKOV: They triumph? Oh, yes. Then they—

PORFIRY: —(finishing Raskolnikov's sentence) Begin executing other people.

RASKOLNIKOV: If necessary. That was quite witty of you.

PORFIRY: Thank you. But tell me, what happens when a quite ordinary person has delusions of grandeur?

RASKOLNIKOV: Oh, that happens quite often. That remark was even more clever than the first.

PORFIRY: Thank you.

RASKOLNIKOV: No reason to. What happens, is this. They will realize they are inadequate, and repent with a beautiful and edifying effect. It's a law of nature.

PORFIRY: Well, that's a consolation. But, are there so many extraordinary people? It might be uncomfortable for the rest of us if there were.

RASKOLNIKOV: Oh, no. Not at all. They are really quite few. Their proportion to the rest of humanity must follow some law of nature, too; but it has yet to be discovered.

ZAMETOV: Are you both joking? Are you making fun of each other?

PORFIRY: No. I think we are in deadly earnest.

ZAMETOV: What horrifies me is that you sanction bloodshed in the name of conscience. To my mind, that is more terrible than the legal sanction of bloodshed.

PORFIRY: Much more terrible.

ZAMETOV: I can't believe you are really serious. I shall read your article.

RASKOLNIKOV: There's only a hint of this in the article.

PORFIRY: What happens if some young man thinks he's another Mahomet and begins removing all obstacles. He has some great enterprise in mind and needs money for it. He decides to get it, do you see?

RASKOLNIKOV: I have to admit that such cases certainly will arise. The young are particularly apt to fall into this snare.

PORFIRY: Well, then?

RASKOLNIKOV: Society has its methods of protecting itself. You have only to catch him.

PORFIRY: And, if we catch him?

RASKOLNIKOV: Then, he gets what he deserves.

PORFIRY: That's logical. But, what of his conscience?

RASKOLNIKOV: What do you care about that?

PORFIRY: Simply for humanity.

RASKOLNIKOV: Well, if he has a conscience he will suffer for his mistake.

ZAMETOV: But, do real geniuses suffer? Oughtn't they

to?

RASKOLNIKOV: That would depend on whether he identifies with his victim. It's not a question of morality, but psychology. A man of large mind must.

PORFIRY: May I ask an impertinent question?

RASKOLNIKOV: Of course.

PORFIRY: While you were writing this article, did you consider yourself to be the least bit extraordinary?

RASKOLNIKOV: Possibly.

PORFIRY: Then could you bring yourself to—?

RASKOLNIKOV: If I did, I certainly shouldn't tell you.

PORFIRY: I was only speaking from a literary point of view.

RASKOLNIKOV: I really can't say. I don't consider myself a Napoleon.

PORFIRY: Oh, come on, don't we all think ourselves Napoleons now?

ZAMETOV: Undoubtedly, it was one of these future Napoleons who did in Alyona Ivanovna last week.

PORFIRY: I must confess I've been thinking along such lines. We must have a long talk, Rodion Romanovitch. Perhaps, you might tell us something.

RASKOLNIKOV: You want to cross examine me in due form?

PORFIRY: Heaven forbid. That's unnecessary. I'm sure Nikolai is innocent, but for the moment, I must hold him until we catch this little Napoleon, whoever he may be. By the way, when you went to deliver your pledge, you saw the painters, didn't you?

RASKOLNIKOV: No, I don't remember any painters. I do remember someone moving out though.

ZAMETOV: What is this? The painters were there on the day of the murder. How could he remember them? Surely—?

PORFIRY: I botched it. I fancied you could have told us something. I'm getting confused.

RASKOLNIKOV: You should be more careful.

ZAMETOV: Look, surely you don't think—

RASKOLNIKOV: It's an old police trick to begin their attack by disarming a suspect into making admissions.

PORFIRY: You imagine that's why I asked you that silly

question. Ha, ha, ha.

RASKOLNIKOV: I'm sick of this! Do you hear?

PORFIRY: Don't get excited. I'm simply a visitor. It's all nonsense. I was just a bit muddled, that's all. I assure you. Do you really think I suspect you? (Raskolnikov glares at him silently) But if I really do, why worry you prematurely? You're a law student; why should I venture to instruct you, considering your sophistication regarding crime? In one case, I may be bound to make an immediate arrest, but in another, why shouldn't I let the suspect wander around for a while. You don't follow me? The point is, if I make an arrest too soon, I may be inadvertently giving our little Napoleon moral support. Ha, ha, ha. You're laughing.

RASKOLNIKOV: Not in the least.

ZAMETOV: Aren't you carrying the joke a little far, Inspector?

PORFIRY: You see, I like to make my proof mathematically clear. Irrefutable. By putting the suspect in jail too soon I deprive myself of getting further evidence against him. How? By setting his mind at rest so he can retreat into his shell. A prosecutor's chief weapon is suspense. You're laughing again? You don't believe me? Ah, you'll learn, you'll learn. There are nerves, Rodion Romanovitch, there are nerves. You overlooked them—in your article, I mean. I hope you don't think I meant that in any other sense, ha, ha, ha? No, I see you don't. Well, what do you make of my theory?

RASKOLNIKOV: It's a lesson.

ZAMETOV: But, what prevents the suspect from running away?

PORFIRY: Where to? To the hinterlands where there are real Russian peasants? Abroad? There are two things a Russian intellectual cannot stand: foreigners and Russian peasants. Psychologically, prison is far more preferable.— To the kind of man I am talking about. Of course, he will lie, but at the last moment, he will weaken. There may be illness, and a stuffy room as well, but nonetheless. What is the matter, Rodion Romanovitch, you look pale? Zametov, open the window.

RASKOLNIKOV: No, no, don't trouble yourself. (to Porfiry) I see quite plainly, that you suspect me of the murder of Alyona Ivanovna and her sister Lizaveta. I'm sick of it. If you wish to prosecute me, arrest me.

(There is a knock at the door.)

ZAMETOV: Aren't you going to answer it?

(The knock is repeated.)

RASKOLNIKOV: May I?

(Raskolnikov opens the door. A workman stands in the doorway and stares at Raskolnikov.)

RASKOLNIKOV: Well? What do you want?

WORKMAN: Murderer!

RASKOLNIKOV: (taken aback, stupefied) W-what?

WORKMAN: Murderer!

(The man turns and leaves. Raskolnikov is visibly shaken.)

PORFIRY: This is some kind of tasteless joke. Go after him, Zametov, and find out who the man is, in the event Rodion Romanovitch wishes to press charges.

ZAMETOV: (hurrying out) Right away.

RASKOLNIKOV: This is your doing.

PORFIRY: Don't be ridiculous.

RASKOLNIKOV: I see what you meant about working on people's nerves. Congratulations.

PORFIRY: Nonsense. I never set eyes on that man before in my life.

RASKOLNIKOV: I won't allow it! (shouting) I won't allow it!

PORFIRY: Good heavens, Rodion Romanovitch, what is the matter with you?

RASKOLNIKOV: I won't allow it,

PORFIRY: Do you want to rouse the neighbors?

RASKOLNIKOV: (mechanically) I won't allow it. I won't allow it.

PORFIRY: If I didn't know you were ill, you'd almost make me suspect you had a guilty conscience. You'll drive yourself mad. Here you are, enraged against destiny and now against the police. Think what may happen. You might confess to a murder of which you are so clearly innocent. And simply because you want to make an end of it.

RASKOLNIKOV: Are you really saying you don't suspect me? Is it possible? Or, are you merely having a little fun?

PORFIRY: Of course I don't suspect you. This is just the aftermath of your delirium.

RASKOLNIKOV: I am not delirious! Do you hear?

PORFIRY: You needn't be so emphatic. If you really were a criminal, would you be so intent on proving yourself in full possession of your faculties? That wouldn't be very clever, would it?

RASKOLNIKOV: You devil. You are trying to show me that you know my game. You want to frighten me. Or worse. You have no other object than to amuse yourself at my expense.

PORFIRY: I genuinely wish you well, my friend. Really, you must take care of yourself. You will frighten your sister.

RASKOLNIKOV: My sister? What has this to do with her? What concern is she of yours?

PORFIRY: Dear boy—

RASKOLNIKOV: I will not allow myself to be tortured.

PORFIRY: I came in quite a friendly way.

RASKOLNIKOV: I spit on your friendship.

PORFIRY: But, I had a little surprise for you. Aren't you interested?

RASKOLNIKOV: If you have grounds to arrest me, do so. If not, GET OUT!

PORFIRY: But aren't you interested in my surprise?

(Zametov returns excitedly.)

PORFIRY: (there is no response from Raskolnikov, turning to Zametov) Well, did you get him?

ZAMETOV: He simply vanished. But I just ran into your clerk. They're looking for you. There's been a development. You are wanted back immediately.

PORFIRY: (excited) Ah. (he looks at Raskolnikov merrily)

ZAMETOV: (glumly) Nikolai has confessed.

PORFIRY: (astounded) What? Now that's a surprise!

RASKOLNIKOV: I suppose you did not expect it.

PORFIRY: You did not expect it either, my friend. See how your hand is trembling! Ha, ha, ha!

RASKOLNIKOV: You must forgive me. I lost my temper.

PORFIRY: Don't mention it. Don't mention it. And we shall meet again; shan't we? Shan't we? Come along, Zametov.

(They leave. Raskolnikov sinks weakly into a chair.)

BLACKOUT/CURTAIN

ACT II

SCENE 4

RASKOLNIKOV'S GARRET

Later that evening. Dounia is pacing up and down, while Razumihin looks out the window.

DOUNIA: (stamping her foot) I can't stand it any longer.

RAZUMIHIN: Calm yourself, Adovtya Romanovna.

DOUNIA: Where can he be?

RAZUMIHIN: I have no idea. Ah, that fool, Zametov. I told him to stay with him.

DOUNIA: (listening) Wait. That must be him.

(There is noise of another door closing.)

RAZUMIHIN: There's a new lodger. He moved in last

night. Poor Rodion, if only he had a wife to care for him. It's his isolation that causes this.

DOUNIA: Yes. A woman would be a great help to him.

RAZUMIHIN: And yet, he loves no one and perhaps he never will.

DOUNIA: You mean he isn't capable of love?

RAZUMIHIN: Not as long as he hates himself.

DOUNIA: (changing the subject) Do you think he intentionally insulted Mr. Luzhin this morning?

RAZUMIHIN: That was pretty obvious.

DOUNIA: I mean, was it his illness, or would he have done it anyway?

RAZUMIHIN: He planned it.

DOUNIA: And what do you think of Mr. Luzhin, Dimitri?

RAZUMIHIN: Well, I confess I didn't care for him. And I don't like the quarters he put you in. But—

DOUNIA: But?

RAZUMIHIN: I'm sure there must be some good in him or you wouldn't marry him. It would be impossible.

DOUNIA: (smiling) Why, thank you, Dimitri. You're very sweet.

RAZUMIHIN: Oh, why I—(he is very confused and falls silent)

DOUNIA: I heard a step.

(There is a knock.)

RAZUMIHIN: Can it be?

DOUNIA: He wouldn't knock.

RAZUMIHIN: (opening the door) Ah. I thought it was Rodya.

LUZHIN: Good evening. I didn't come to see Rodion Romanovitch. I thought his sister might be here.

RAZUMIHIN: She is. Come right in.

LUZHIN: (to Dounia) I couldn't find you at your rooms, and I learned from your landlady that you had gone to your brother's.

DOUNIA: (graciously) You are very welcome, Pyotr Petrovitch.

LUZHIN: (stiffly) I trust you had a pleasant journey?

DOUNIA: Oh, very. And you?

LUZHIN: (as before) Very. Do you find your lodgings to your taste?

DOUNIA: They are very clean and neat.

LUZHIN: I'm glad. Your brother expressed some reservations about them.

DOUNIA: I should like to introduce you to Dimitri Prokovitch Razumihin. He has been a treasure to me.

LUZHIN: I've had the pleasure. (silence) Where is your brother?

DOUNIA: He's gone out. He'll be back soon.

LUZHIN: (smirking) Ah.

DOUNIA: Did you know that Madame Svidrigailov is dead?

LUZHIN: To be sure. I have it on good authority that her husband has arrived in Saint Petersburg.

DOUNIA: Svidrigailov! Here?

LUZHIN: Yes. He probably arrived last night.

DOUNIA: Why won't he leave me in peace?

LUZHIN: I don't think he will bother you, unless, of course, you wish to see him. I don't know where he's lodging yet, but I'll find him.

DOUNIA: I'm convinced that he murdered his wife.

LUZHIN: It's impossible to prove that now. But it's certain he was capable of it. As a matter of fact, I helped to hush up some homicidal brutality on his part at the time of his marriage.

DOUNIA: Was there evidence of this?

LUZHIN: I said I was involved in the matter. Or didn't you hear me? (softening) What happened was this. Svidrigailov was involved with a young woman. She was pregnant and had been talking of trying to prevent the marriage. One day she was found hanging. The verdict was suicide. But that verdict might never have been reached but for lavish expenditures by Madame Svidrigailov.

DOUNIA: Are you saying it was murder?

LUZHIN: Not precisely. Foul play could not exactly be proved. Yet death by suicide was by no means certain, since the girl did not seem inclined that way. And then there was the case of a man servant who died of ill treatment some years ago.

DOUNIA: I don't know that. That was a suicide, no question about it, I'm told.

LUZHIN: A suicide, yes. But Svidrigailov drove him to it.

DOUNIA: When I was there he always behaved well towards the servants and they did not seem to blame him for the man's death.

LUZHIN: I perceive, Adovtya Romanovna that you are disposed to defend him. There's no doubt he has a way with the ladies.

DOUNIA: Say no more about him, I beg you. It makes me miserable.

LUZHIN: If you prefer. (pause) Shouldn't your brother be coming back? He shouldn't leave you unchaperoned with Mr. Razumihin for so long.

DOUNIA: Pyotr Petrovitch!

RAZUMIHIN: You dare to suggest? Don't you dare—

LUZHIN: Nothing of the kind. I merely am remarking it's not exactly the behavior of a thoughtful brother who respects the conventions.

DOUNIA: I know you quarreled, but don't allow your anger to say something beneath you. Rodya will apologize if he was at fault.

LUZHIN: Do you doubt it? I didn't come here to insult him. There are insults which no patience can bear; there are lines which cannot be overstepped.

DOUNIA: That wasn't what I meant. Don't you understand our whole future depends now on whether all this is explained and set right as soon as possible? If you have any regard for me, you must end this matter today.

LUZHIN: That's a strange way to put it. It seems to me I can have a high regard for you and dislike some member of your family.

DOUNIA: Don't be so ready to take offense. Be the sensible and generous man I've always thought you to be, and wish to think you. Don't you see, if this cannot be settled amicably I must break off with you? I shall learn if he is a brother to me or not; and I shall learn whether I am respected and dear to you or not. I want to know these things.

LUZHIN: I find that offensive. Do you set me on the same level as that impertinent boy?

DOUNIA: What! You are offended at my placing you beside all that is most precious in my life? You are offended at my taking too little account of you?

LUZHIN: Love of your future husband ought to outweigh your love for your brother. In any event, he clearly doesn't respect you enough to chaperone you. He leaves you here with a stranger.

RAZUMIHIN: This is an outrage.

DOUNIA: He's angry. He doesn't mean it.

LUZHIN: Where is your brother? Don't you know?

DOUNIA: He—he's gone out. He was sick. If you must know I am frantic.

LUZHIN: There's nothing to worry about. I'm sure he's in good hands.

DOUNIA: What do you mean? Do you know where he is?

LUZHIN: No. But I know where he was. Don't trouble yourself about him.

DOUNIA: Where is he? Where is he? Speak!

LUZHIN: As you know I am lodging with Mr. Lebziatnikov. In the same building, there are several tenants including a family that is nearly destitute. The daughter is a streetwalker. The father is a drunkard by the name of Marmeldov. Well, it so happens that Marmeldov was run over by a carriage this afternoon. Your brother seems to have known him; at any rate he brought him home. Marmeldov was still alive, but died soon after. Your brother was very solicitous of the family, and gave all his money to the daughter, who will, I am sure, make good use of it. In any event, he decided to console her and took her off somewhere. No doubt he will not hesitate to introduce her to you.

DOUNIA: I don't believe you. How do you know this?

RAZUMIHIN: If you were not betrothed to this lady, I'd—

DOUNIA: How do you know it? How?

RAZUMIHIN: My friend Lebziatnikov was present. He told me. When your brother's name was mentioned I asked for details. There is no mistake.

DOUNIA: There must be.

LUZHIN: See for yourself. Here they are now.

(And indeed, Raskolnikov and Sonya have entered. They are unaware they are the subject of the conversation. Sonya is pretty but she is not a flaming harlot. Still, she has the air of a woman who can be bought, although the purchase might not be an unalloyed pleasure, for she is a miserable girl. All turn to look at them.)

RASKOLNIKOV: Ah, Dounia, I want to introduce you to Sonya Semyonovna.

RAZUMIHIN: I wouldn't have believed it.

RASKOLNIKOV: This is my sister Adovtya Romanovna.

DOUNIA: (ashen) I am very pleased to meet you.

SONYA: (confused) And I'm very pleased to meet you.

LUZHIN: This is an outrage. I won't permit it.

RASKOLNIKOV: What won't you permit?

LUZHIN: How dare you introduce this woman to my fiancée? After all, she's your sister, too.

RASKOLNIKOV: To my thinking, for all your virtues, you're not worth the little finger of this unfortunate girl.

LUZHIN: And neither is your sister, I take it. I don't care what you think of me. But have you no respect for her? You introduce your paramour to your sister, after having bought this woman's affection hardly two hours before.

RASKOLNIKOV: That's a lie.

LUZHIN: Is it? Did you not empty your pockets to this girl this afternoon?

RASKOLNIKOV: I don't know where you get your information from, but you are misinformed. I gave money to her family to pay for her father's funeral. He died in an accident which I witnessed this afternoon.

LUZHIN: Well, perhaps I am misinformed. But if a tryst was not your purpose, why bring her to your rooms, may I ask? Was that necessary?

RASKOLNIKOV: I wanted to talk to her.

LUZHIN: Ah, is that what they call it now?

RASKOLNIKOV: Dog!

LUZHIN: You can see for yourself whether it's possible for us to agree?

DOUNIA: I think you had better explain, Rodya. Pyotr Petrovitch is angry, and perhaps unjust, but—

RASKOLNIKOV: I shall explain nothing to him. Nothing whatever.

LUZHIN: Come, Adovtya. Let's not come between lovers. Let's not be indiscreet.

DOUNIA: I intend to stay until Rodya explains.

LUZHIN: Come away, now. If I leave without you, I shall consider myself released.

DOUNIA: You seem to consider your wishes as commands. I am not under your authority, even though I've thrown up everything to come here, relying on you.

LUZHIN: That's not quite true. You received a small legacy from Madame Svidrigailov. Very apropos, considering the tone you are taking with me.

DOUNIA: I take it, from that remark, that you are relying on my helplessness.

LUZHIN: In any case, I can no longer, and I certainly don't wish to interfere. No doubt Mr. Svidrigailov's proposals are more to your liking, if your taste is similar to your brother's.

RASKOLNIKOV: Aren't you ashamed now, sister?

DOUNIA: I am ashamed, Rodya. Pyotr Petrovitch, go away.

LUZHIN: If I do, I shan't come back. Remember what you are saying.

DOUNIA: What insolence! I don't want you to come back.

LUZHIN: What! Is that how it is? I could reproach you with justification.

RAZUMIHIN: What right have you to speak to her like that? What can you protest about? What rights have you?

LUZHIN: But you agreed; and now you break it off— And I have had expenses— (Raskolnikov laughs)

RAZUMIHIN: (furious) Expenses? What expenses are you talking about, you fool? Those rooms; she's paying for them herself!

DOUNIA: Enough, Dimitri, no more, please. Pyotr Petrovitch, be kind enough to go.

LUZHIN: I'm going. But you seem to forget I was about to marry you despite your reputation. I thought you might be grateful. Evidently, I acted recklessly in disregarding the universal verdict.

RAZUMIHIN: Do you want your head smashed?

DOUNIA: You are a mean and spiteful man!

RASKOLNIKOV: (restraining Razumihin) Leave this room at once.

LUZHIN: (going up to Sonya) You're the cause of all this, you slut. Well, there are laws dealing with your kind. I'll be revenged upon (to Raskolnikov) you through her. I'll have your little sweetie taken up.

RASKOLNIKOV: If you dare—

(But Luzhin is gone.)

RAZUMIHIN: Let me go after him.

DOUNIA: No, don't. It would only make matters worse.

RASKOLNIKOV: At least, sister, you are not to be without defenders.

DOUNIA: What do you mean?

RASKOLNIKOV: Why, I mean that Dimitri here—

RAZUMIHIN: I'll brain you.

RASKOLNIKOV: Look at him blush.

RAZUMIHIN: Nothing of the sort. What do you mean? Nonsense!

DOUNIA: Leave Dimitri alone, Rodya. Where have you been all this time? It's been hours.

RASKOLNIKOV: Been? Been?

DOUNIA: Yes. Why did you leave when you knew Dimitri had gone to fetch me?

RASKOLNIKOV: Ah, I can't tell you.

DOUNIA: What do you mean you can't tell me? Why can't you tell me?

RASKOLNIKOV: It will only upset you unnecessarily.

DOUNIA: Rodya, I'm your sister.

RAZUMIHIN: What did Zametov do? I'll bet it was his fault.

RASKOLNIKOV: Come here a moment, Dimitri, I want to talk to you privately.

RAZUMIHIN: Well, what happened? What is it?

RASKOLNIKOV: You mustn't tell my sister.

RAZUMIHIN: Very well.

RASKOLNIKOV: Zametov was here. Then a Police Inspector came. He knew that I was present in the tavern when Nikolai proposed killing that old woman for her money.

RAZUMIHIN: So that's why you were so interested in that murder.

RASKOLNIKOV: The Inspector pretended he only wanted to question me about it informally. But that was only a pretext.

RAZUMIHIN: A pretext!

RASKOLNIKOV: He suspects me.

RAZUMIHIN: How could he? Is he mad?

RASKOLNIKOV: Oh, he made it very clear; but then he denied it, of course. Then, right in the middle of the discussion a man knocks on the door. I open it. He looks at me and says, Murderer! then runs off. It was the Inspector's doing, I'm sure of it. He wanted to frighten me.

RAZUMIHIN: But they can't do this. I have relatives in the department. We shall complain.

RASKOLNIKOV: Ah, but that's not all. News came that Nikolai had confessed.

RAZUMIHIN: Well, then that's all over.

RASKOLNIKOV: I don't think so. The Inspector is still sure I am the killer. Soon we shall hear that Nikolai has recanted and the game will begin again.

RAZUMIHIN: Why? He has a confession. What does he want?

RASKOLNIKOV: How should I know? Maybe I fit his theory better. At any rate, I'm sure I'm still under suspicion.

RAZUMIHIN: Ah, it's insulting, insulting. How dare they? But why did you run off?

RASKOLNIKOV: I was very upset, delirious again, I

think. Then I saw Marmeldov run down by a carriage. That sobered me up.

RAZUMIHIN: And the girl?

RASKOLNIKOV: I needed someone to talk to.

RAZUMIHIN: Ah, I understand. That Luzhin is a scoundrel.

DOUNIA: (fed up) Well, Rodya, are you going to answer me now or not?

RASKOLNIKOV: There's nothing I can tell you.

DOUNIA: Then apparently I am not wanted here.

RASKOLNIKOV: Perhaps, it would be better for us to part for a time.

DOUNIA: Good God!

RAZUMIHIN: Brother, what are you doing to your sister?

DOUNIA: Are you throwing me out, Rodya?

RASKOLNIKOV: I'll come to you when all this is over—if I can. Don't come to me. It would be better to forget me.

DOUNIA: (running out) Wicked, heartless egoist.

RAZUMIHIN: How could you?

RASKOLNIKOV: Go after her. But don't tell her anything. It's easier this way.

(Razumihin goes out. Raskolnikov sinks down. Sonya comes forward.)

SONYA: I don't understand. I am to blame for this.

RASKOLNIKOV: No, not you. I am.

SONYA: You have hurt your sister terribly.

RASKOLNIKOV: I know that.

SONYA: Yet you love her very much.

RASKOLNIKOV: More than anything. I have only you now. I've come to you. We are both cursed. Let's go away together.

SONYA: Go where?

RASKOLNIKOV: How do I know? I only know we must take the same road.

SONYA: I can't leave my family now. They need me more than ever. Only, only—after what you did for us today, if it were up to me alone, I would follow you to the ends of the earth.

RASKOLNIKOV: I need you more than they do.

SONYA: I don't understand. I only know you are suffering.

RASKOLNIKOV: Why are you standing up? Sit down.

(Sonya finds a seat.)

RASKOLNIKOV: How thin you are.

SONYA: I've always been like that.

RASKOLNIKOV: Even when you lived at home?

SONYA: Yes.

RASKOLNIKOV: Of course you were. Your father told me all about you. How you went out and came back with the money, and how Katerina Ivanovna begged you to forgive her. He told me she used to beat you.

SONYA: Oh, no. What are you saying? No.

RASKOLNIKOV: You love her then?

SONYA: Love her? Of course. And if she did hurt me, what then? What of it? You know nothing about it. She is so unhappy. She is like a child. She is good.

RASKOLNIKOV: What will happen to you? They were on your hands before. What now?

SONYA: I don't know. The landlady wants to throw her out and Katerina Ivanovna says she doesn't want to stay another minute.

RASKOLNIKOV: So bold? Is she depending on you?

SONYA: Oh, no. Don't talk like that. We are one. We live like one. You smile? Aren't you sorry for them? How can I tell them you gave them your last penny?—It's not as though I haven't been cruel to them myself.

RASKOLNIKOV: You?

SONYA: Last week I bought some fancy handkerchiefs from Lizaveta the peddler. I showed them to Katerina and she wanted me to give her one. But I wouldn't. For spite.

RASKOLNIKOV: You knew Lizaveta?

SONYA: Yes, did you? (silence)

RASKOLNIKOV: Katerina Ivanovna has consumption. She will soon die.

SONYA: Oh, no, no, no.

RASKOLNIKOV: It will be better if she dies.

SONYA: No, not better. Not better at all!

RASKOLNIKOV: And the children? Will you take them to live with you?

SONYA: Oh, I don't know.

RASKOLNIKOV: And what if, even while Katerina is alive, you fail? What will happen then?

SONYA: How can you? That cannot be!

RASKOLNIKOV: Cannot be? I suppose you've taken insurance against it?

SONYA: God will not let it be.

RASKOLNIKOV: Have you been able to save for a rainy day?

SONYA: No.

RASKOLNIKOV: Have you tried?

SONYA: Yes.

RASKOLNIKOV: And it didn't work! Of course not! No need to ask. (pause) You don't get money every day?

SONYA: No.

RASKOLNIKOV: It will be the same for your sister.

SONYA: No-o! It can't be! She's just a baby. God would not allow anything so awful.

RASKOLNIKOV: She's how old? Eleven. He lets others come to it at that age.

SONYA: God will protect her.

RASKOLNIKOV: And if there is no God?

SONYA: What are you doing to me?

RASKOLNIKOV: You know what your worst sin is, Sonya?

SONYA: Yes, I know.

RASKOLNIKOV: Being a prostitute, right? No. Your worst sin is that you've ruined yourself for nothing. Living in this filth, which you loathe, doesn't help anyone. Wouldn't it be better to end it all?

SONYA: What would become of them?

RASKOLNIKOV: What will become of them in any event? Or is it that vice is not as loathsome to you as before?

SONYA: No. I hate it more than ever.

RASKOLNIKOV: Then are you out of your mind? Do you expect a miracle? Do you pray for a miracle?

SONYA: All the time.

RASKOLNIKOV: You pray to God a lot, eh?

SONYA: (eyes shining) What should I be without God?

RASKOLNIKOV: Ah, that's it. And what does God do for you?

SONYA: Be silent! Don't ask! You don't deserve—

RASKOLNIKOV: That's it! That's it!

SONYA: He does everything.

RASKOLNIKOV: So that's your way out. That's your explanation. You're a religious maniac. (Sonya begins to cry quietly) What if Luzhin makes good his threat to have you arrested? What then? (Sonya tries to reply but cannot) Imagine Sonya. Katerina Ivanovna and the children will die of starvation and your sister will follow you into the street.— Suppose it were up to you whether Luzhin or they will perish. How would you choose?

SONYA: Why do you ask what cannot happen?

RASKOLNIKOV: So it's better for Luzhin to live and do evil? You don't dare to decide even that? I thought you had the strength to transgress. You've destroyed a life, your own to be sure, but you've taken that life.

SONYA: You're crazy. Who am I to judge who is to live or die? I don't know Divine Providence.

RASKOLNIKOV: Once Divine Providence is mixed in it, there's no doing anything.

SONYA: Are you simply trying to torture me? Say straight out what you're leading up to.

RASKOLNIKOV: You've got to look life in the face, not just say God won't allow it.

SONYA: (back to crying) What is to be done? What is to be done?

RASKOLNIKOV: Break what must be broken once and for all. The goal is freedom and power. Power over all creation, over the whole miserable ant-heap. (she continues to cry) Ah, what's the use? Why do I keep torturing you?

SONYA: Oh, how you are suffering.

RASKOLNIKOV: Do you know who killed Lizaveta?

SONYA: That student. They've caught him.

RASKOLNIKOV: Nikolai is innocent. The real murderer is still at large.

SONYA: Then how do you know about it?

RASKOLNIKOV: Guess.

SONYA: But you? Why do you frighten me like this?

RASKOLNIKOV: I must be a great friend of his since I know. Nikolai spoke of murder, talked about killing the old woman the night before at a tavern. I was there, so was your father. But one of those men committed the murder. The man who did it didn't mean to kill Lizaveta; just the old woman. But Lizaveta walked in. It was unintentional.

SONYA: (forlorn, helpless) Not my father.

RASKOLNIKOV: Can't you guess then? Take a good look. (Sonya retreats) Have you guessed?

SONYA: Good God. What have you done? What have you done to yourself? (Sonya hugs him and weeps)

RASKOLNIKOV: You're a strange girl. Why do you kiss me?

SONYA: There is no one. There is no one in the whole world as unhappy as you are.

RASKOLNIKOV: Then you won't leave me?

SONYA: No. No. Never! I will follow you everywhere. I will follow you to Siberia.

RASKOLNIKOV: Perhaps I don't choose to go to Siberia.

SONYA: How could you? A man like you? How could you bring yourself to do it?

RASKOLNIKOV: Forget it. Let it alone.

SONYA: Were you so hungry, so desperate?

RASKOLNIKOV: That's not why I did it. Don't torture me, Sonya.

SONYA: And the money you gave us today, is that—?

RASKOLNIKOV: No. No, that was my own. As for what I took from the old woman, I hid that. Actually, I don't know if there is any money in it. I didn't have time to look at it. I hid it under a loose flagstone in Saint Sylvester's churchyard.

SONYA: Then why did you rob if you took nothing?

RASKOLNIKOV: I haven't quite decided whether to take the money or not. If I'd done it simply from hunger I'd be happy now. But I'm a coward and a mean wretch.

I should never have told you. We are so different.

SONYA: No, it's a good thing. It's better I should know. Far better. Tell me, I'll understand. I'll understand in myself.

RASKOLNIKOV: You'll understand? We shall see. It was like this. I asked myself what Napoleon (gesturing towards the bust) over there would do if he were in my place? Would he have hesitated?

SONYA: You'd better tell me straight out.

RASKOLNIKOV: It's very simple. In ten or twelve years, I might, with luck, have got a job as a teacher with a salary worth a pittance. By then my mother would be worn to grief. My sister—well, my sister might have fared worse, and my youth would be over. And then what? Marry and die and leave the world as penniless as I came into it. I wanted to do something decisive. Action had to be taken. So I resolved to kill that voracious old witch. It was as simple as that. I've only killed a louse, Sonya, a useless, harmful creature.

SONYA: A human being,—a louse!

RASKOLNIKOV: From the moral point of view.

SONYA: And Lizaveta?

RASKOLNIKOV: I'd like not to think about that. But it

was an accident. Ah, that's not it either. I could have managed without doing any of this. Others have. Razumihin will. So should I. But I preferred to sit here staring at the wall for days. It was then I discovered mankind isn't worth the effort. And I realized whoever is strong in mind and spirit will have power over people. He who despises them most will be a law giver among men. It's always been so and it always will be so. It's a law of nature. A man must be blind not to see it. And no one has ever seen it. No one. That's why I did it. I wanted to have the daring.

SONYA: Oh, hush, hush. You have turned away from God, and God has smitten you and given you over to the devil.

RASKOLNIKOV: (amused) You really think this revelation of mine was inspired by the devil?

SONYA: Don't blaspheme. You don't understand.

RASKOLNIKOV: If I really was Napoleon, would I have had to ask myself if the old woman was a human being or a louse? The very question proved I wasn't up to it. Don't you see, it wasn't the money I wanted. Don't you see? I had to prove I was a being with the right to kill— or if not, if not, then I was no better than anybody else, and just as much a louse as anybody else.

SONYA: (aghast) To kill. To have the right to kill.

RASKOLNIKOV: That, or admit I was a louse like all the rest. And that's it, you see. I'm not up to it. I am a louse, and someone has the right to snuff me out as remorselessly as I snuffed out her life.

SONYA: And you murdered her!

RASKOLNIKOV: I murdered myself, not her. Up till then I could always believe I was a man. That I had the right to transgress, to step over barriers, even if I chose not to. I could always rationalize and say I choose to obey the law.

SONYA: This is awful.

RASKOLNIKOV: Let me be, Sonya. Let me be.

SONYA: What suffering.

RASKOLNIKOV: What am I to do now?

SONYA: What are you to do? Go at once to the nearest crossroad, kiss the earth and confess. Ask God's forgiveness. Then God will send you life again. Will you go? Will you go?

RASKOLNIKOV: You mean I should give myself up?

SONYA: Suffer and expiate your sin. That's what you must do.

RASKOLNIKOV: No. I will not go to them. Don't be a child, Sonya. Why should I go to the authorities? They destroy men by the millions and look on it as a virtue. They are knaves and scoundrels. And justice is only an illusion, a chimera. No. They have no right to judge me.

SONYA: It will be too much for you to bear. Too much.

RASKOLNIKOV: Perhaps I'm a little hasty in condemning myself. Perhaps I'm a man and not a louse after all.

SONYA: What a burden to bear! And your whole life. Your whole life.

RASKOLNIKOV: I'll get used to it. Anyway, the police are on my track.

SONYA: Oh, no.

RASKOLNIKOV: Why be upset? You want me to go to Siberia, don't you? They shall arrest me soon; but they don't have enough evidence. I'll be in prison for a time.

SONYA: Do you have a cross on you?

RASKOLNIKOV: No.

SONYA: Here, take mine. It was once Lizaveta's. We exchanged crosses. I shall suffer with you.

RASKOLNIKOV: Give it to me.

SONYA: I will come and visit you.

RASKOLNIKOV: It might be better if you didn't.

SONYA: I thought you wouldn't want me to.

RASKOLNIKOV: Perhaps I will. Sonya, go away now. I want to be alone. Please be a good girl. Come tomorrow, but leave me alone now.

SONYA: I'll come tomorrow.

(She leaves. Raskolnikov lies down staring at the ceiling. The wall next to Napoleon shows a series of slide flashes.)

1st. Raskolnikov wandering up and down a series of endless stairs.
2nd. A bare garret room.
3rd. Raskolnikov searching for something.
4th. Raskolnikov finding an old lady hiding behind a chair, doubled up.
5th. Taking out the ax and chopping her.
6th. The old woman seems to be made of wood or stone.
7th. He hits her again.
8th. Nothing happens.
9th. The old lady is laughing.
10th. She is rocking back and forth.
11th. There are hundreds of little old ladies.

(The door opens. A man has stood there watching Raskolnikov. Raskolnikov was aware of his presence.)

RASKOLNIKOV: Don't you believe in knocking?

MAN: I knew you weren't asleep.

RASKOLNIKOV: Well, who are you? What do you want?

MAN: I'm your next door neighbor. I just moved in last night.

RASKOLNIKOV: Ah, yes. Well, you still haven't said what you want?

MAN: Why, merely to make your acquaintance. Allow me to introduce myself: Arkady Ivanovitch Svidrigailov.

RASKOLNIKOV: Am I still dreaming? Nonsense! You can't be he!

SVIDRIGAILOV: But I am, I assure you, Rodion Romanovitch. I've come both because I should like to know you and because I hope you will assist me in a matter relating to your sister.

RASKOLNIKOV: I'm afraid I'm about to disappoint you.

SVIDRIGAILOV: I see no reason to justify myself, but what is so reprehensible on my part in this business? That I made infamous proposals to a defenseless girl and insulted her? But, I was offering her all I could offer while my wife was alive. What wrong have I committed but to fall in love? Is it my fault that your sister was a little child completely unknown to me when I married my wife? The question is, am I a monster, or am I a victim?

RASKOLNIKOV: But that's not the point. Whether you are monster or a victim, we dislike you. We show you the door.

SVIDRIGAILOV: There's no getting around you. I thought I would but you take the right line at once.

RASKOLNIKOV: But you're still trying to get round me.

SVIDRIGAILOV: What of it? What of it? Is there anything wrong with that? There would never have been any unpleasantness if my wife hadn't—

RASKOLNIKOV: The rumor is you got rid of her, too.

SVIDRIGAILOV: You've heard that nonsense? Well, you'd be sure to. My conscience is quite at rest on that score. Legally, the case is closed. Now, as to the moral point of view—

RASKOLNIKOV: Do you trouble yourself about that?

SVIDRIGAILOV: I only struck her twice. She was actually delighted. The story about your sister had been wrung to the last drop. No one to gossip with any more, when suddenly those blows fell from heaven. Her first reaction was to order the carriage.

RASKOLNIKOV: You fought a lot?

SVIDRIGAILOV: Oh, no. Actually we got on quite well. Only twice in all our seven years. I'm rather adaptable.

RASKOLNIKOV: Too adaptable.

SVIDRIGAILOV: Because I'm not offended by your rudeness? But why take offense? I could crush you easily enough if I chose. I haven't talked to anyone in several days. I'm delighted to talk to someone. I'm not such a bear, you know.

RASKOLNIKOV: I fancy you're a man of good breeding, or at least know how to act like one if the occasion serves.

SVIDRIGAILOV: I'm not particularly interested in anyone's opinion of me and therefore why not be vulgar at times; vulgarity is such a convenient cloak for our climate, especially when one has a natural propensity that way.

RASKOLNIKOV: I've heard you were a gambler.

SVIDRIGAILOV: No, my dear boy. I was a card sharper.

That was how my wife got hold of me. She bought up all my debts and then proposed to me. She made me sign an I.O.U. for 30,000 roubles. Ah, I fancy if all women were like my wife there would be little nonsense in the world.

RASKOLNIKOV: And you did it?

SVIDRIGAILOV: Obviously. Why not? You can't always get rid of your debts and marry a beautiful woman at the same time. She was beautiful and I was attracted. Only last year she gave me back my I.O.U. After seven years of marriage. You see how much she trusted me. (laughing)

RASKOLNIKOV: You seem to miss her.

SVIDRIGAILOV: I do. She was a good woman. But then I'm not altogether alone. Do you believe in ghosts?

RASKOLNIKOV: What sort of ghosts?

SVIDRIGAILOV: Just ghosts.

RASKOLNIKOV: Do you?

SVIDRIGAILOV: Well— Marfa Petrovna is pleased to visit me.

RASKOLNIKOV: What?

SVIDRIGAILOV: Three times since the funeral.

RASKOLNIKOV: Were you awake?

SVIDRIGAILOV: Quite. She appears, then she goes out the door. The same door.

RASKOLNIKOV: Does she speak?

SVIDRIGAILOV: Yes.

RASKOLNIKOV: What does she say?

SVIDRIGAILOV: Oh, just nonsense. And she was such a sensible woman. It's sad to think she had degenerated since her death.

RASKOLNIKOV: I was thinking of the same sort of thing that's happening to you. I wonder why?

SVIDRIGAILOV: What! Did you really? I knew we had something in common. Didn't I tell you so?

RASKOLNIKOV: You never said so.

SVIDRIGAILOV: Are you sure? I thought I did. When I came in and saw you pretending to be asleep, I said to myself, Here's the man.

RASKOLNIKOV: What do you mean by that?

SVIDRIGAILOV: What do I mean? I really don't know.

RASKOLNIKOV: But, perhaps you are telling lies.

SVIDRIGAILOV: I rarely lie. But tell me, do you believe ghosts exist?

RASKOLNIKOV: No. I won't believe that.

SVIDRIGAILOV: People generally say you are ill when you see them. That doesn't prove they don't exist; it merely proves that only sick people can see them. If you believe in a future life, it seems to me you could believe in ghosts, too.

RASKOLNIKOV: I don't believe in a future life.

SVIDRIGAILOV: And what if there were only spiders there? We always picture eternity as vast. But why? Suppose it's one little room like a bath house with spiders everywhere. I sometimes imagine it that way.

RASKOLNIKOV: Can it be you imagine nothing more comforting than that? Or more just?

SVIDRIGAILOV: How do you know that wouldn't be just? It's what I certainly would have made it.

RASKOLNIKOV: (with an involuntary shiver) Look, what did you come here for?

SVIDRIGAILOV: Why in such a hurry?

RASKOLNIKOV: We all have our plans.

SVIDRIGAILOV: Whatever you do, don't give in. Don't surrender.

RASKOLNIKOV: (puzzled) What? What are you talking about?

SVIDRIGAILOV: Oh, nothing really. Just advice in general. You appear despondent.

RASKOLNIKOV: (losing patience) Will you stop beating around the bush and come to the point?

SVIDRIGAILOV: Very well. It regards your sister.

RASKOLNIKOV: You lack the right to mention her to me.

SVIDRIGAILOV: Please. Don't be such a prig. We are men of the world. Let us act so. You need have no fear on her account. Nor am I about to say something that could reflect on her. She is most damnably chaste. At first, you know, my wife began confiding family secrets to her. She had that despicable habit. At any rate, she told her all the dark rumors about me.

RASKOLNIKOV: I've heard that you caused the death of a young girl.

SVIDRIGAILOV: Don't refer to such vulgar tales.

RASKOLNIKOV: I was told, too, about a serf of yours—

SVIDRIGAILOV: I beg you to drop the subject. (silence) Your sister began to pity me. She wanted to reform me. Of course, I was eager to be reformed by her. That was my plan. She constantly sermonized me. Ah, what the passion for propaganda will bring some girls to! I almost succeeded, but I botched it. I was too eager. To what a pitch of stupidity a man can work himself up to. Never undertake anything in a frenzy, Rodion Romanovitch. But, perhaps you have cause to know this already?

RASKOLNIKOV: You keep hinting at something. Look, why did you come to Petersburg in the first place?

SVIDRIGAILOV: To prevent Dounia from marrying that scoundrel, Luzhin.

RASKOLNIKOV: That's already been accomplished.

SVIDRIGAILOV: I know that.

RASKOLNIKOV: How could you know?

SVIDRIGAILOV: The walls are thin my friend and you were all shouting at the top of your lungs.

RASKOLNIKOV: Perhaps you heard other things as

well?

SVIDRIGAILOV: It's possible.

RASKOLNIKOV: So you listen at doors.

SVIDRIGAILOV: Expound the latest theories, dear boy, do! One mustn't listen at doors, but one may murder old women at one's pleasure. What a prankster you are! The modern generation isn't depraved, it's simply whimsical.

RASKOLNIKOV: What do you mean to do? Inform the police?

SVIDRIGAILOV: I'm not an informer.

RASKOLNIKOV: Then what do you want from me?

SVIDRIGAILOV: I want to see your sister. I am going on a journey to America very soon, and before I go, I want to give her some money.

RASKOLNIKOV: I can't be blackmailed into that.

SVIDRIGAILOV: I'm not trying to blackmail you. I told you what I know merely so that we understand each other. In the first place, my wife left her some money. I also wish to make amends for the trouble I caused her. The fact I speak openly about it should make it clear my intentions are honorable. Well, what do you say?

RASKOLNIKOV: No, I won't.

SVIDRIGAILOV: Then I'll be forced to try and see her myself, and upset her by doing so.

RASKOLNIKOV: I'm sure you still have designs on her.

SVIDRIGAILOV: Now that's a quaint expression! Designs on her! Seriously! Your sister can't endure me.

RASKOLNIKOV: That's not the point.

SVIDRIGAILOV: Are you sure of that? She doesn't love me, but that doesn't mean she's unwilling to see me. Will you swear she regards me with aversion?

RASKOLNIKOV: Are you daring to suggest?

SVIDRIGAILOV: Men don't fall in love with a woman that loathes them. That's a female trick—

RASKOLNIKOV: And if I tell her you want to see her; will you promise not to try to see her if she refuses?

SVIDRIGAILOV: I should very much like to see her.

RASKOLNIKOV: Can't you control your weakness? Have you lost the strength to stop yourself?

SVIDRIGAILOV: Do you pretend to strength of character?

RASKOLNIKOV: You are nothing but a roué and an eavesdropper.

SVIDRIGAILOV: But what else is there to do, Rodion Romanovitch? I am bored and but for this I might have to shoot myself.

RASKOLNIKOV: Could you?

SVIDRIGAILOV: Please don't speak of it. I admit it's an unpardonable weakness, but I can't help it. I am afraid of death and I dislike talking about it. Have no fear that I will use the information I have to blackmail you. I am a man, not a louse. Come. You will see, we'll be great friends.

(Svidrigailov smiles and leaves as unceremoniously as he entered. After he leaves, Raskolnikov walks to the bust of Napoleon.)

RASKOLNIKOV: My God, why have you forsaken me?

CURTAIN

ACT III

SCENE 5

RASKOLNIKOV'S GARRET

A few days later.

DOUNIA: (entering hurriedly) Rodya. Rodya where are you? (she puts down several packages)

SVIDRIGAILOV: (entering quietly behind her) He's gone out. Everyone's gone out except me, Dounia.

DOUNIA: (reacting to his voice as to an electric shock) You!

SVIDRIGAILOV: Why so surprised? It's not as if you didn't know I live here.

DOUNIA: Where is Rodya?

SVIDRIGAILOV: Wandering about some place. Probably with Sonya. Her step-mother died, I believe.

DOUNIA: He hasn't been to see me at all.

SVIDRIGAILOV: And you haven't been to see me. Why are you frightened like a child? Am I really so terrible?

DOUNIA: Though I know you're not a man of honor, I am not the least afraid of you.

SVIDRIGAILOV: And you're not in the least curious as to what I may know about your brother? You got my letter?

DOUNIA: Here is your letter. You hint at a crime committed by my brother. You hint it clearly. You don't deny it now. But I already heard this from Mr. Razumihin. It's nonsense. That's why I hesitated to come.

SVIDRIGAILOV: I have the most certain proofs.

DOUNIA: You can have no proofs. It's a disgusting and ridiculous suspicion. Speak, go ahead. But let me tell you I don't believe you. I don't believe you.

SVIDRIGAILOV: Then why do you risk staying with me alone? The house is deserted. Why wait for an explanation, if you're sure it's false? Surely you're not curious to the point of folly?

DOUNIA: Don't torment me. Tell me! Tell me!

SVIDRIGAILOV: There's no denying you are a brave girl. Shall I lock the door? We don't want to be interrupted. (he does with no protest from Dounia) Well? Are you afraid now? You really are brave.

DOUNIA: Stop playing games with me about this. What proof have you?

SVIDRIGAILOV: The wall separating this room from mine is very thin. I heard him confess to that girl, Sonya, that he is the murderer. He killed the old pawnbroker woman and her sister. He took the money and hid it under a loose rock in Saint Sylvester's churchyard. That's all I know. There's no need to worry. Sonya is in love with him. She won't betray him.

DOUNIA: It cannot be. It cannot be. There's no motive. It's a lie. It's a lie.

SVIDRIGAILOV: The motive was robbery. And he did rob her although he has no idea how much he stole. That's because his courage failed him.

DOUNIA: But, how could Rodya steal or rob? Can he be a thief?

SVIDRIGAILOV: A thief? No. But a murderer, yes. You yourself find it harder to believe him a thief than a murderer!

DOUNIA: (accusingly) But you said the motive was robbery!

SVIDRIGAILOV: Ostensibly. But the real motive was a theory. A theory that divides mankind into superior men who can do what they want, and inferior ones who must obey the law because of their inferiority. Add to that the knowledge that, but for the lack of a paltry sum of money, his whole career would be brilliant. Mix in the obvious fact that a mean, totally worthless old woman has that money and a lot more. What could you expect? Right at the moment, he is suffering from the knowledge that, although he was able to formulate his theory, he lacked the guts to boldly overstep the law. That proves he is no genius. He finds that very humiliating.

DOUNIA: But remorse? Doesn't he have remorse?

SVIDRIGAILOV: Not at present. That will depend on whether he can salvage his pride or give up his theory. Right now he's still convinced his theory is correct. But the problem is, he isn't one of the elect. He finds that painful.—You are very pale, Dounia.

DOUNIA: I know his theory. He wrote an article in a magazine. Of course, I read it.

SVIDRIGAILOV: That will make it even more difficult for him to save face, for an intellectual to take a public position and be forced to recant.— (Dounia starts to leave, Svidrigailov becomes agitated) Where are you going?

DOUNIA: I want to see Sonya. How do I find her?

SVIDRIGAILOV: She's probably with your brother. Best see her alone. Calm yourself, Dounia. Believe me, he has friends. We will save him. Would you like me to take him abroad? He will do many good deeds in the future to atone for the murder. He may become a great man yet.

DOUNIA: Cruel man! To jeer at him. (staring to go) Let me go to him. Where is he? Why is this door locked?

SVIDRIGAILOV: (reasonably) We can't have uninvited guests walking in while we're having a discussion like this. I am far from jeering at your brother. But, how can you leave here in such a state? You will upset him and he will give himself up. Do you want to betray him? He can still be saved. Let us consider this calmly. Do sit down.

DOUNIA: (sitting down) How can you save him? Can he really be saved?

SVIDRIGAILOV: That depends on you. On you alone.

DOUNIA: (back on her feet) What do you mean?

SVIDRIGAILOV: You. One word from you and he is saved. I—I'll save him. I love you beyond everything. Let me kiss the hem of your dress. Let me, let me. The very rustle is too much for me. Say "Do that" and I'll do that. Don't! Don't look at me like that. Don't you know you are killing me?

DOUNIA: Open it! Open it! (calling) Is there no one there?

SVIDRIGAILOV: There's no one. It's a waste of time to shout like that. You are only agitating yourself uselessly.

DOUNIA: Where's the key? Open the door at once! At once!

SVIDRIGAILOV: I've lost it and I can't find it.

DOUNIA: This is an outrage.

SVIDRIGAILOV: If it were to come to that I am at least twice as strong as you. You couldn't complain afterwards, either. Not unless you're willing to expose your brother. And then, it's very difficult to prove an assault. That way, even if you sacrifice your brother, you might prove nothing.

DOUNIA: Coward!

SVIDRIGAILOV: As you like. But please observe I am only speaking hypothetically. Violence is hateful to me. I was only trying to show you that, in that situation, you need have no remorse—should you decide to save your brother of your own accord. You would only be submitting to violence. His fate is in your hands. I will be your slave all my life. I will marry you. I'm going to sit down and wait for your decision (Dounia pulls a pistol from her purse) Aha! So that's it, is it? Well that alters matters completely. That makes things wonderfully easy for me. But where did you get the revolver? Ah, why it's an old one of mine.

DOUNIA: It's not yours. It belonged to your wife, like everything else in your house. You killed her, and if you take another step, I swear I'll kill you.

SVIDRIGAILOV: What about your brother? Just curious.

DOUNIA: Inform if you want to! Don't stir! Don't come near me! I'll shoot. You poisoned your wife, I know you did. You are a murderer yourself.

SVIDRIGAILOV: Are you so positive I poisoned her?

DOUNIA: You did. You've hinted at it yourself. I know you bought some poison. It must have been your doing. It must have.

SVIDRIGAILOV: If that were true, you would have been the cause. It would have been for your sake.

DOUNIA: You are lying! I've hated you. Always. Always.

SVIDRIGAILOV: Tsk, tsk. You seem to have forgotten how you behaved in the heat of propaganda. I saw it in your eyes. Do you remember that moonlight night when the nightingale was singing?

DOUNIA: That's a lie! That's a lie and a libel!

SVIDRIGAILOV: A lie? Well, if you like I made it up. Women mustn't be reminded of such things. (advancing) I know you will shoot, you wild thing. (advancing) I've never seen you so beautiful—

(She fires and grazes his hair line.)

SVIDRIGAILOV: (delighted) My kitten has scratched me. She has claws. She aimed straight at my head. What's this? Blood? (wiping it with his handkerchief as if it were a treasure) But you missed! Don't be so nervous with your next shot. Fire again. I'll wait until you've reloaded. (silence) Well, if you go on like this I'll have time to dance a mazurka before you're ready to shoot again.

DOUNIA: Let me be. I swear I'll shoot again. I—I'll kill you.

SVIDRIGAILOV: Well, at this range you can hardly help it. But if you aren't going to…. (she pulls the trigger, but the gun misses fire; Svidrigailov takes the gun from her) Here. I thought I taught you how to load it. (loading it) Now, you see, you must do it like this. Here, try again. (giving the gun back to her)

DOUNIA: You—you'd sooner die than give me up?

SVIDRIGAILOV: That's apparent, isn't it?

(Dounia drops the gun. He comes and takes her into his arms. She makes no resistance but cries.)

DOUNIA: Let me go.

SVIDRIGAILOV: Then, you don't love me? (Dounia shakes her head) And, you can't? (she nods) Never? (she nods)

DOUNIA: Never! I'm sorry, Arkady, I wish I could. I truly do.

SVIDRIGAILOV: Here is the key.

DOUNIA: Poor Arkady, how you must love me.

SVIDRIGAILOV: Take it. Go, quickly.

DOUNIA: What will you do now, Arkady?

SVIDRIGAILOV: Perhaps I shall go to America. Yes, today in fact.

DOUNIA: In all this rain?

SVIDRIGAILOV: If you're going to America you don't let yourself be stopped by rain. Go, Dounia! Go now, while I still have self control.

DOUNIA: Goodbye, Arkady. (she goes out without another word)

SVIDRIGAILOV: (picking up the revolver, he begins spinning the chamber) Let's see if you are properly loaded? Aha, my beauty. We will need you if we are going to America. (smiling) Going to America.

(Svidrigailov goes back to his room. The stage remains empty for a short time and then Raskolnikov enters wearily. He sits down.)

RAZUMIHIN: (entering) So I've finally found you. I was here earlier. Where have you been?

RASKOLNIKOV: I've been walking by the river.

RAZUMIHIN: As far as I'm concerned you may go to hell.

RASKOLNIKOV: You're drunk.

RAZUMIHIN: Maybe so, brother, maybe so. All I've come for is to find out for sure if you're mad or not. I don't want to know your precious secrets. All I know is that you've made your sister miserable beyond words, and—

RASKOLNIKOV: When did you see her?

RAZUMIHIN: This morning. She made up her mind to come and see you; she wouldn't allow me to come with her. (seeing the packages) Aha, she's been here and gone. Don't you realize she's convinced you're more interested in that girl Sonya than in her? She's started calling Sonya your girl. I don't know what she is to you, but I went to see her today and there she was, trying on mourning dresses; she said you hadn't been to her at all. So you're mad. Only I'd—

RASKOLNIKOV: I've never seen you drunk before, Dimitri. It becomes you.

RAZUMIHIN: (rising) Goodbye.

RASKOLNIKOV: I was talking to my sister about you.

RAZUMIHIN: When?

RASKOLNIKOV: A few days ago.

RAZUMIHIN: What did you say to her—I mean about me?

RASKOLNIKOV: I told her you're a good, honest man. I didn't tell her you love her because—

RAZUMIHIN: Thank God!

RASKOLNIKOV: Because she doesn't need to be told.

RAZUMIHIN: She knows?

RASKOLNIKOV: It's pretty obvious. I know you will look after her the way I want her to be looked after. I want you to tell her that I'm sorry for all the pain I've caused her and that I shall always love her.

RAZUMIHIN: You're so mysterious. I am sure this is some nonsense. No doubt, you're a political conspirator, and—

RASKOLNIKOV: It's better that, for a while, you don't know.

RAZUMIHIN: If you've drawn her into some plot—

RASKOLNIKOV: Nonsense. There's no plot. Listen, Dimitri, she'll need help when I am gone.

RAZUMIHIN: You talk as if you were going to prison.

RASKOLNIKOV: Maybe I am. It's very likely.

RAZUMIHIN: What nonsense. Look, I'm leaving. I can't make any sense of it and you're obviously not going to explain. You know, if Nikolai hadn't confessed, I'd almost think that you— Well, never mind. Goodbye. (Razumihin goes out)

RASKOLNIKOV: Now I must settle with Svidrigailov.

PORFIRY: (entering) You weren't expecting a visitor, Rodion Romanovitch?

RASKOLNIKOV: Sit down Inspector, sit down.

PORFIRY: I passed your friend on the stairs, but he didn't see me. I hid on the landing below.

RASKOLNIKOV: Well? What do you want? (silence) Why don't you say something?

PORFIRY: Ah, these cigarettes. Dreadful habit. But I can't give them up. My doctor warned me about my lungs, but what's the use?

RASKOLNIKOV: Why, you're up to your tricks again. Why are you here?

PORFIRY: I've come here to have it out with you. I owe you an explanation and I must give it to you. I've decided openness is better between us. Before Nikolai confessed, I was firmly convinced that you—well—

RASKOLNIKOV: You paid that man to call me a murderer.

PORFIRY: Yes, I confess it, I was counting on your excitability. I had great hopes for you at that moment.

RASKOLNIKOV: But what are you driving at now?

PORFIRY: It's caused you a great deal of suffering. I am not a monster. I realize what it must mean for a proud, impatient man to bear such treatment! You are a man of noble character. I liked you from the first. I want to do all I can to efface the original impressions I created in you. I am speaking sincerely.

RASKOLNIKOV: Then you no longer believe I am guilty.

PORFIRY: It's no longer necessary to go into every detail. It was just one thing after another. You were the only one not to claim your pledges. You were present when Nikolai spoke of the crime. You knew that he would call for Lizaveta at seven o'clock. You were taken ill the day after the murder. All of that proves nothing, and yet—Well, you can't blame a lawyer for being partial to his own theory. And then there was your article, Rodion Romanovitch, there was your article. Why, it all fitted perfectly. Forgive my jeering at your article. I really liked it. It was bold, youthful, incorruptible.

RASKOLNIKOV: And the man? Was he necessary?

PORFIRY: You see, I had nothing but conjecture. I needed a little fact. Here is my little fact, I thought. When Nikolai confessed I couldn't believe it. I didn't want to believe it. And I thought, here is Nikolai, a student, but a child, really. A show-off, a boaster. Enthusiastic enough, but his ideas aren't really formed. Not formed enough for him to act on them. I've come to like Nikolai, and I'm studying him in detail. Pretty soon he's going to recant his confession.

RASKOLNIKOV: What!

PORFIRY: He can't hold out. He answered plausibly enough. But he's not the murderer. No. The murderer looks upon himself as an honest man, and he poses as injured innocence. No, that's not the work of Nikolai.

RASKOLNIKOV: Then who is the murderer?

PORFIRY: Who is the murderer? (whispering) Why, you are Rodion Romanovitch. You are the murderer. (silence) Your lip is twitching as it did before. When the man I hired called you a murderer. You've been misunderstanding me. That's why you're so surprised. I came on purpose to tell you and deal openly with you.

RASKOLNIKOV: It was not I who murdered her.

PORFIRY: It was you, Rodion Romanovitch, you and no one else.

RASKOLNIKOV: You are up to your tricks again.

PORFIRY: Oh, stop. We are alone. There are no witnesses. Why not be frank with each other? I haven't come to ensnare you.

RASKOLNIKOV: Then what did you come for? If you're sure, why not arrest me? I ask you again.

PORFIRY: In the first place, I haven't quite enough evidence. In the second place, because I don't want you to think of me as a monster. And finally, because I think you will confess.

RASKOLNIKOV: What if you are wrong?

PORFIRY: No. I have a little fact.

RASKOLNIKOV: What little fact?

PORFIRY: Something that will enable me to arrest you before long. I shan't tell you when. For the time being you may run around loose.

RASKOLNIKOV: Why should I confess when, as you yourself have previously hinted, I will gain moral support from being arrested.

PORFIRY: Don't you see a confession would lessen your sentence? It would weigh heavily in your favor, especially since another man has taken the guilt on himself. I swear I will not mention that I ever suspected you for an instant.

RASKOLNIKOV: No. It isn't worth it. I don't care a rap

about lessening the sentence.

PORFIRY: That's what I was afraid of. Ah, don't disdain life. So much of it lies before you.

RASKOLNIKOV: A great deal of what lies before me?

PORFIRY: Life. You've lost faith and you think I'm mocking you. But how old are you? How much do you understand? You invented a theory and it turned out to be base; now you're ashamed. Don't be. You haven't lost your honor entirely. It's well you only killed those two old women. God knows what you might have done if you had invented another theory. Annihilated a race, a class, a civilization. You're lucky to have so little blood on your hands. If you repent, in time, you'll live down what you have done. You're not afraid of the punishment; that would be shameful. You don't see the justice in it yet, but you will. You will. What you need is fresh air, fresh air, fresh air.

RASKOLNIKOV: But who are you? What kind of prophet are you? From what majestic height do you proclaim these words of wisdom?

PORFIRY: I'm an old man whose life is over. Look, even if they send you to prison for twenty years, you'll come out ten years younger than I am. Perhaps you think I am trying to get around you by flattery. Well, perhaps I am. But I am trying to help you.

RASKOLNIKOV: And what if I run away?

PORFIRY: You won't! Where can you go? What you need more than anything is a definite position. Only we can give you that. You can't get on without us.

(There is a shot from Svidrigailov's room.)

RASKOLNIKOV: Good heavens, Svidrigailov.

PORFIRY: We'd best see about that.

(They go out. The stage remains empty. There is noise in the adjoining room. Then Sonya enters. She goes to the bed and sits on it. She has obviously not heard the shot. Porfiry and Raskolnikov enter.)

PORFIRY: Just fancy. Making you his heir. Well, I must report this. And Rodion Romanovitch, if you should choose to take his way, leave a note explaining why. It would be more generous.

(Raskolnikov turns and comes into the room.)

SONYA: Rodya!

RASKOLNIKOV: You're here, Sonya!

SONYA: You haven't been to see me, so I came to you.

RASKOLNIKOV: I'm glad you came. But I don't know

why you should come. I'm a contemptible person.

SONYA: You are suffering more now than before, aren't you?

RASKOLNIKOV: Yes. To escape disgrace I thought of drowning myself in the river, but I decided if I considered myself strong, I'd better not be afraid of disgrace.

SONYA: Pride, Rodya.

RASKOLNIKOV: You don't think that I was simply afraid of the water?

SONYA: Oh, darling, hush.

RASKOLNIKOV: I am going to give myself up. But I don't know why.

SONYA: To atone for your crime by suffering.

RASKOLNIKOV: Crime! What crime? That I killed that vile old woman, that insect? Killing her was atonement for forty sins. I am not thinking of expiating it.

SONYA: Oh, Rodya.

RASKOLNIKOV: I'm not even sure that I am not going to confess because there's an advantage in doing so. As was suggested. Oh, the imbecility of my cowardice!

SONYA: Rodya, Rodya, what are you saying? You've shed blood.

RASKOLNIKOV: All men shed blood; it flows and always has flowed in torrents; men are crowned with laurels and called benefactors of mankind for shedding blood. Look at it clearly, Sonya, and understand. I wanted to be a benefactor of mankind. I mean that sincerely. I would have made up for this little stupidity by so many acts of greatness. No, it's not stupidity. THE IDEA WAS NOT STUPID! It only seems that way now that it has failed. The fault was not in the idea, but in me. If I had succeeded, I would have been crowned with glory. Now, I'm simply trapped.

SONYA: But that's not so, not so. What are you saying?

RASKOLNIKOV: It's not picturesque; not aesthetically attractive. Napoleon hiding under an old woman's bed. I realize how insipid, grotesque and even base it seems. But I fail to see how bombarding people by regular siege is more honorable. Fear of appearances is the first sign of impotence. I've never recognized this more clearly than now. And I'm further than ever from seeing that what I did was a crime. No, the reasoning was correct. Everything is permissible.

SONYA: And you are going to give up like this? Oh, don't, don't.

RASKOLNIKOV: It was you who wanted me to. Why is

it you are frightened now it's about to happen?

SONYA: But I didn't want this. I wanted—

RASKOLNIKOV: Ah, yes, you are a religious maniac.

(Silence. Sonya weeps.)

RASKOLNIKOV: Ah, forgive me. I am wicked. But why are you so fond of me when I clearly don't deserve it? Oh, if I were alone and loved no one. Nothing of all this would ever have happened. If only I had been a cynic and not loved mankind. Ah, what an irony.

SONYA: (firmly) You will repent, Rodya.

RASKOLNIKOV: I doubt it. Anyway, I am going. But I won't go to the Inspector. I won't give him the satisfaction. Now what are you crying for again? It's your wish. Leave off, will you! Oh, how I hate it all.

SONYA: Say at least one prayer first.

RASKOLNIKOV: Sorry, I can't.

SONYA: I'll come with you.

RASKOLNIKOV: No, stay here. What's the use of going in procession? I'll go alone.

SONYA: Someday, you will repent, Rodya. I'll be waiting.

RASKOLNIKOV: Who knows? Anything is possible with a contemptible creature like me. But, will that prove that I'm right then and wrong now? My spirit may be broken then and I may believe in all sincerity that it's morally right to be a louse. But does the fact I've changed prove it? Does it? Goodbye, Sonya. (he goes out dejected, but firm)

SONYA: Au revoir, my love. You'll repent. I know you will.

(She takes an icon out of her bag and lights a candle under it, near the bust of Napoleon. The lighting makes the little Corsican appear to be positively smirking.)

CURTAIN

ABOUT FRANK J. MORLOCK

FRANK J. MORLOCK has written and translated many plays since retiring from the legal profession in 1992. His translations have also appeared on Project Gutenberg, the Alexandre Dumas Père web page, Literature in the Age of Napoléon, Infinite Artistries.com, and Munsey's (formerly Blackmask). In 2006 he received an award from the North American Jules Verne Society for his translations of Verne's plays. He lives and works in México.

Printed in Great Britain
by Amazon.co.uk, Ltd.,
Marston Gate.